THE LANGUAGE OF PROSE

By the same authors

THE LANGUAGE OF POETRY

The Language of Prose

by

ROBERT MILLAR, M.A.
Moray House College of Education

and

IAN CURRIE, M.A., M.Litt., F.E.I.S.
Moray House College of Education

HEINEMANN EDUCATIONAL BOOKS

LONDON AND EDINBURGH

Heinemann Educational Books Ltd

LONDON EDINBURGH MELBOURNE AUCKLAND TORONTO
HONG KONG SINGAPORE KUALA LUMPUR
IBADAN NAIROBI JOHANNESBURG
NEW DELHI

ISBN 0 435 10571 X

Published by
Heinemann Educational Books Ltd
48 Charles Street, London W1X 8AH
Printed in Great Britain by
Morrison & Gibb Ltd, London and Edinburgh

Contents

Preface

This introduction to the practical criticism of prose is a companion volume to *The Language of Poetry*. By the practical criticism of prose we mean the close and detailed analysis of relatively short pieces of writing, extracts from novels, short stories, essays, articles, scientific treatises, etc., in order to determine how the writer obtains certain effects; his deployment of his linguistic resources, his selection of language and syntactical patterns, his arrangement and structuring of ideas in order to achieve most effectively his purpose in writing.

The range of prose is so vast that it is only possible in a handbook of this kind to consider in any detail a few of the principal uses to which prose can be put. We shall therefore concentrate in the main on two kinds of prose – discursive prose, used in the exposition of ideas, and creative or imaginative prose.

In recent years a great deal of work has been done in investigating and analysing the general linguistic features of many of the varieties of prose we come across in daily life – religious language, scientific exposition, advertising, and so on. Attention, however, perhaps needs to be focussed on some of the subtler methods by which writers can manipulate the responses of their readers. In general, interpretation and comprehension exercises for schools have tended to concentrate far too narrowly on the purely referential aspects of meaning, what the words of a passage refer to, the factual meaning of a passage. In the process a good many of the most powerful effects of successful writing have tended to be neglected. This applies not only to literary prose in the widest sense but also to scientific and technical prose. Some of the most essential and desirable qualities of good expository writing are the lucidity and coherence with which an argument or explanation is presented. The analysis of the processes lying behind the achievement of these qualities is just as valuable and rewarding as the explanation of the aesthetic effects of more literary writing.

A book such as this can do no more than suggest a few approaches which will perhaps illuminate the techniques used in the successful deployment of language in prose, so that the reader can evaluate prose for himself. The importance of the evaluation of prose cannot be exaggerated. In a world in which we are constantly assailed by prose writing, much of it carefully designed to manipulate our minds and condition us to the writer's way of thinking, where language is used as a weapon, an important part of the armoury of the educated person is a knowledge of at least some of the techniques used in communication. Skill in practical criticism may help to develop a healthy critical awareness of the written or spoken word. The study may make the difference between mere unthinking prejudice and beliefs founded on informed and reasoned judgements.

At the same time it is to be hoped that the reader will not only be helped to a finer, more satisfying, and more discriminating appreciation of the art of the writer but will also gain some aid in the effective handling of language himself.

R. M.

I. C.

Acknowledgements

The authors and publishers wish to thank the following for permission to reprint copyright material:

The Executors of the James Joyce Estate and Jonathan Cape Ltd for extract from *The Dead* from *The Dubliners*; the Trustees for the Copyrights of the late Dylan Thomas and J. M. Dent & Sons Ltd for extract from *Under Milk Wood*; The Bodley Head for extract from *The Great Gatsby* from *The Bodley Head Scott Fitzgerald*, Vol I; Harold Pinter and Methuen & Co. Ltd for extract from *The Caretaker*; The Estate of Lewis Grassic Gibbon and Hutchinson & Co. Ltd for extract from *Sunset Song* from *A Scots Quair*; Laurence Pollinger Ltd and the Estate of the Late Mrs Frieda Lawrence for extracts from *The Rainbow*, *The White Peacock*, *The Complete Short Stories* and *Sons and Lovers* by D. H. Lawrence; The Bodley Head for extract from *Talk About America* by Alistair Cooke; Macmillan & Co. Ltd for extract from *The Last Enemy* by Richard Hillary; Basil Willey and Chatto & Windus Ltd for extract from *The Eighteenth Century Background*; Her Majesty's Stationery Office for extract from Winston Churchill's Speech to Parliament, *Hansard* 4th June, 1940; The Executors of the Ernest

Hemingway Estate and Jonathan Cape Ltd for extracts from *A Farewell to Arms*; the Literary Estate of William Faulkner and Chatto & Windus Ltd for extract from *Intruder in the Dust*; Brian H. Kirman and The Rationalist Press Association Ltd for extract from *This Matter of Mind*; Lord David Cecil and Constable & Co. Ltd for extract from *The Young Melbourne*; Curtis Brown Ltd and John Dos Passos for extract from *The 42nd Parallel*; Richard Hughes and Chatto & Windus Ltd for extract from *The Fox in the Attic*; Peter Forster and Eyre & Spottiswoode Ltd for extract from *Play the Ball*; The Executors of the Estate of Sir James Fraser for extract from *The Golden Bough* (abridged edition); The Trustees for the Joseph Conrad Estate and J. M. Dent & Sons for extract from 'Youth' from *Typhoon and Youth* and from *The Nigger of the Narcissus*; Mrs Laura Huxley and Chatto & Windus Ltd for extract from 'Music at Night' by Aldous Huxley; Mrs Sonia Brownell and Secker & Warburg Ltd for extract from 'Politics and the English Language' from *Collected Essays, Journalism and Letters*; Miss Rose Elton and Chatto & Windus Ltd for extract from *A Writer's Notes on His Trade* by C. E. Montague; John Updike and André Deutsch Ltd for extract from *Pigeon Feathers and Other Stories*; Mrs A. S. Strachey and Chatto & Windus Ltd for extracts from *Elizabeth and Essex* and *Queen Victoria* by Lytton Strachey; Faber & Faber Ltd for extract from *Lord of the Flies* by William Golding; The Literary Estate of V. Sackville-West and The Hogarth Press for extract from *The Edwardians*; Norman Mailer and Weidenfeld & Nicolson Ltd for extract from *Miami and the Siege of Chicago*; Edward Arnold for extract from *A Passage to India* by E. M. Forster; The Literary Estate of Virginia Woolf and the Hogarth Press for extract from *Orlando*; the Society of Authors as the Literary representative of the Estate of Katherine Mansfield for extract from 'The Lady's Maid'; Weidenfeld & Nicolson Ltd for extract from *A Legacy* by Sybille Bedford; Macmillan & Co. Ltd for extract from *Historical Essays* by Hugh Trevor-Roper; Routledge & Kegan Paul Ltd for extract from *Satellites and Scientific Research* by Desmond King-Hele; Hamish Hamilton Ltd for extract from *American Capitalism* by J. K. Galbraith; The Longman Group Ltd for extract from *The History and Philosophy of Science* by L. W. H. Hull; A. D. Peters & Co. for extract from 'First Confession' by Frank O'Connor from *The Stories of Frank O'Connor*.

PART ONE

I

What Practical Criticism Works With

Whereas the assured described in the Schedule hereto has contracted with the ———— Assurance Company Limited (hereinafter called 'the Company') for the following assurance upon the basis of a proposal the date of which is specified in the Schedule.

Now this Policy Witnesseth that in consideration of the payment having been made to the Company on the first premium particulars of which are stated in the Schedule the Company hereby covenant that if the subsequent premiums shall be paid in manner prescribed in the Schedule then upon proof being given to the reasonable satisfaction of the Directors of the Company of the happenings of the event or of more than any one of the events specified in the Schedule the Company will pay in London to the person or persons specified in the Schedule the sum specified in the Schedule together with such further sum or sums as may be appropriated by way of bonus in addition thereto.

Insurance Policy

Now the word of the Lord came unto Jonah the son of Amittai, saying, 'Arise, go to Nineveh, that great city, and cry against it; for their wickedness is come up before me.'

But Jonah rose up to flee unto Tarshish from the presence of the Lord, and went down to Joppa; and he found a ship going to Tarshish so he paid the fare thereof and went down into it, to go with them unto Tarshish from the presence of the Lord.

The Bible

Although the vast majority of crystalline substances have no useful ductility at ordinary temperatures, those which do have tend to be altogether too ductile. Pure crystals of iron, silver, gold and so on, are too soft to be of much practical use and the art and science of metallurgy consists very largely in making such crystals harder and stronger without making them too brittle.

The New Science of Strong Materials

Yes, the newspapers were right: snow was general all over Ireland. It was falling on every part of the dark central plain, on the treeless hills, falling softly upon the Bog of Allen and, farther westward, softly falling into the dark mutinous Shannon waves. It was falling, too, upon every part of the lonely churchyard on the hill where Michael Fury lay buried. It lay thickly drifted on the crooked crosses and headstones, on the spears of the little gate, on the barren thorns. His soul swooned slowly as he heard the snow falling faintly through the universe and faintly falling, like the descent of their last end, upon all the living and the dead.

JAMES JOYCE, *The Dead*

These extracts are all examples of a few of the many different varieties of English prose. As such they are the raw material on which practical criticism, or informed close reading, works. If you add examples from your own day-to-day reading matter, you will see at once that prose is called upon to perform a vast array of tasks in written communication. It is the world's maid of all work. Each extract above is, at a cursory glance, clearly different from the others, and yet you may not be able to recognize, except in a rather vague way, the special features which distinguish one kind of writing from the others, nor to decide how good of its kind each one is.

The purposes behind the pieces of writing are varied and this is reflected in differences in the rhythm, grammatical structure and syntax, and in vocabulary. The aim of practical criticism is to enable you to evaluate and compare stretches of prose by providing the necessary critical apparatus and techniques. As Raymond Williams has succinctly put it, we are concerned with 'who says what to whom with what effect and why'.

At first glance it would seem that the close reading and analysis of prose ought to be a much simpler and easier process than the practical criticism of poetry since, in general, poets tend to handle language in a highly original or idiosyncratic way. Paradoxically, however, it is pre- cisely this difference between the language of poetry and the language of prose which makes the latter so much more difficult to analyse effectively. One might say that the language of poetry is 'opaque' while the language of prose is 'transparent'. By this we mean that the language of poetry draws attention to itself; we are conscious of the words as words. This is what Mallarmé implied when he made the seemingly obvious statement that poetry is made of words; he was drawing our attention to one of the characteristics of poetry – that we are consciously aware of the poet manipulating our responses through the medium of language. The poet invites us, as it were, to examine and admire the techniques with which he obtains his effects.

In prose, on the other hand, this is not generally the case. We seem to look through the words directly to the things which they describe; hence the use of the term 'transparent'. We are not normally conscious of the words themselves but only of the objects and events to which the words refer. The novelist, for example, seems to create a mock-world and it is this we are aware of when we are reading a particular novel, and it is this we remember rather than the way he has handled language in creating this simulacrum of reality. Therefore in evaluating a novel we tend to think in terms of plot and characters and setting. We may, of course, go on to discuss a particular novelist's 'style', a critical term which is very difficult to define, since if it means anything, it means the linguistic techniques he uses to present his particular vision of the world. We therefore find ourselves in the long run going through the same processes as in the practical criticism of poetry.

If a novelist's style becomes obtrusive, however, if our attention is distracted from what he is saying to the way in which he is saying it, we tend to regard it as a fault. Story tellers who have paid too much attention to flourishes of style, like John Lyly in *Euphues* in the sixteenth century or Walter Pater in *Marius the Epicurean* in the nineteenth, receive a mention in the literary histories but few people other than literary scholars read them. Having said that, one must immediately qualify it by noting that one of the most stylistically mannered novels of all time, James Joyce's *Ulysses*, is perhaps a twentieth-century masterpiece. Posterity will decide.

Conversely, some novelists guilty of lapses in style and taste have written works of considerable impact in spite of their occasional clumsiness of expression. Theodore Dreiser, for example, an American novelist writing at the beginning of this century and largely self-educated, was guilty of perpetrating glaring grammatical solecisms. In his novel *Sister Carrie* there occurs the following sentence: 'All day and night it snowed and the city began to suffer a general blockade (sic) of traffic'; and the disregard for conventional morality of the protagonist of *The Financier* is described in these terms: 'It never occurred to him that he could not or should not like other women at the same time. There was a great deal of palaver about the sanctity of the home. It rolled off his mental sphere like water off the feathers of a duck.' The visual image conjured up by the 'mental sphere' of the last sentence is odd, to say the least. Nevertheless, both *Sister Carrie* and *The Financier* are novels of considerable power in spite of their stylistic defects.

Most great novelists, however, have been good stylists as well, for as Gibbon, the eighteenth-century historian said, 'Style is the image of character'. Paradoxically, however, their art is the art that conceals art, which is why the practical criticism of prose, even literary prose, is more difficult than that of poetry. The novelist, through his use of language, in the creation of characters, descriptions of events and so on, manipulates our responses just as effectively as the poet, but, because his effects tend to be large-scale effects, we are not immediately aware of them. If a novel is successful, we are usually so absorbed in the development of the action that it is only perhaps at a second or third reading that we begin to appreciate the techniques used by the author.

As is so often the case in questions of literary theory, Coleridge went to the heart of the matter when he said:

> The words in prose ought to express the intended meaning, and no more; if they attract attention to themselves it is, in general, a fault ... in verse you must do more; there the words, the media, must be beautiful, and ought to attract your notice ... Some prose may approach towards verse, as oratory, and therefore a more studied exhibition of the media may be proper; and some verse may border on mere narrative, and there the style should be simpler.

As an illustration of Coleridge's statement that where we are conscious of the language of prose the prose is usually approaching the condition of poetry, let us look at the prose used in Dylan Thomas's radio play, *Under Milk Wood*, which begins with a voice saying very softly:

> To begin at the beginning:
> It is spring, moonless night in the small town, starless and bible-black, the cobble-streets silent and the hunched courters' – and-rabbits' wood limping invisible down to the sloeblack, slow, black, crowblack, fishingboat – bobbing sea. The houses are blind as moles (though moles see fine tonight in the snouting velvet dingles) or blind as Captain Cat there in the muffled middle by the pump and

the town clock, the shops in mourning, the Welfare Hall in Widow's weeds, and all the people of the lulled and dumbfound town are sleeping now.

This carefully cadenced prose with its exploitation of the sound effects of the English language, its marked use of alliteration, and play upon words inhabits that border region where prose imperceptibly fades into poetry. Try making a list of all the devices of language which strike you as being more characteristic of poetry than prose. Would you still accept the passage as prose, and, if so, why?

Up till now we have been contrasting poetry only with the novel; we have been comparing the language of poetry and *literary* prose. In daily life, however, most of the prose we come in contact with is non-literary. Income Tax forms, pamphlets, newspaper articles of all kinds covering everything from sport to politics, speeches, sermons, business and personal letters, literary or music criticism, historical or sociological works, technical books, guide books, scientific dissertations—all these use prose as their medium; all have more in common with each other (and the novel and drama) than with poetry. The purpose of this kind of prose is broadly informative and most of it is, of course, ephemeral and not worth the bother of close analysis. Sometimes, however, the quality of the thought and the writing in journalism or a historical work, for instance, can invest a work with a more permanent literary appeal. Gibbon's *The Decline and Fall of the Roman Empire* is now probably read more as a superb piece of literary prose than as a historical document, as is Macaulay's *History of England*, since the historical accuracy of both is probably suspect.

Everything we have said of the language of the novel applies equally to the other forms of non-literary prose. We are normally too concerned with the flow of ideas or the development of an argument to want to be distracted by the language itself. Good prose, of any kind, more often than not works by stealth.

THE SPECTRUM OF LANGUAGE USAGE

Basically the ways in which we use language fluctuate between two extremes characterized by I. A. Richards in his *Principles of Literary Criticism* as the *scientific* use of language and the *emotive* use of language.

A statement may be used for the sake of the reference, true or false, which it causes. This is the *scientific* use of language. But it may also be used for the sake of the effects in emotion and attitude produced by the reference it contains. This is the *emotive* use of language.

Richards later moved on to a more subtle theory of the relationship between language and meaning for, as formulated here, it tends to suggest that there are two and only two ways of using language. However, if it is recognized that he was describing the extreme positions, the distinction is a useful one. It had, indeed, been anticipated by De Quincey whose division of literature into two kinds contains hints of Richards' categories:

> There is first the literature of *knowledge*; and secondly the literature of *power*. The function of the first is – *to teach*: the function of the second is – *to move*: the first is a rudder: the second an oar or sail.

Poetry, particularly lyric poetry at the one extreme, exploits the emotive use of language, using words for their connotations and colour, their associations and sound, their emotive charges and overtones. It is highly subjective and personal. Scientific prose, at the other extreme, tries to confine itself as far as possible to the referential aspect of meaning, it eschews emotion and value judgements. It is objective and impersonal. At one extreme is the cry from the soul of the lyric poet: at the other the cold abstract symbols of mathematics. (Even these in certain circumstances may take on emotional overtones. Who could ever hear now without some emotional reverberation the equation $e = mc^2$, the formula which was the theoretical foundation of the atomic bomb?)

Between these poles of the lyric and mathematical symbolism we will find all sorts and shades of prose, exploiting the two basic uses of language in varying degrees. The recognition, examination, and analysis of the varieties is one of the aspects of the practical criticism of prose.

THE DISTINCTION BETWEEN CONVERSATION AND
SPOKEN PROSE

Since many extracts of prose selected for close analysis may well contain passages of dialogue, one distinction ought to be made clear at the outset, that between conversation and spoken prose. As Professor Abercrombie points out in his *Studies in Phonetics and Linguistics*, conversation is spoken language, what we use when we communicate orally with our fellow human beings, converse with our family or friends, or talk with officials or public servants. What we read, however, in passages of dialogue in novels or hear spoken in plays on the stage is not conversation but *spoken prose*, and this is much further from the conversation of real life than most people imagine. What seems 'naturalistic' is in fact very artificial and artistic. As Professor Abercrombie says:

. . the truth is that nobody speaks at all like the characters in any novel, play, or film. Life would be intolerable if they did; and novels, plays or films would be intolerable if the characters spoke as people do in real life. Spoken prose is far more different from conversation than is usually realized.

This can be very easily illustrated by comparing a piece of genuine conversation with dialogue from a novel and a play. The first extract is part of the transcript of a recorded conversation between three educated people:

A: I always find the sports page best entertainment. On Monday I read that . . .
B: I can't stand football reports.
A: Can you not?
B: Apart from Peterborough.
C: Peterborough has a team, has it?
B: Pardon?
A: What?
C: What division is it in?
A: Third. It's the top, still top, isn't it?
B: Yes, been top for about two months.
A: Why isn't it in the second? Oh, just two months.
B: Yes.
A: Not the end of the season yet, that's the reason.
B: And it'll be bottom of the second all next season.
A: Will it?

This passage is fairly typical of genuine conversation in that, while the general drift is clear enough, it proceeds in an inconsequential way, sentences remain unfinished, essential parts of the grammatical structure are omitted, and there are syntactical variations which look odd on the printed page but which would not be noticed as unusual when spoken.

On the other hand, any passage of dialogue from a novel, however close to real conversation it may seem, shows evidence of careful structuring by the novelist, of selection of significant detail, and of a tighter grammatical structure than is generally found in the authentic spoken word. This example from Scott Fitzgerald's *The Great Gatsby* catches the tone of genuine conversation but is designed with superb artistry to fulfil its purpose of giving us an insight into the character of Gatsby, an American *nouveau riche* who has accumulated a fortune by dubious means. The incident takes place in 'the high Gothic library panelled with carved English oak' during a party in Gatsby's house.

A stout, middle-aged man, with enormous owl-eyed spectacles, was sitting somewhat drunk on the edge of a great table, staring with unsteady concentration at the shelves of books. As we entered, he wheeled excitedly around and examined Jordan from head to foot.

'What do you think?' he demanded impetuously.

'About what?'

He waved his hand toward the book-shelves.

'About that. As a matter of fact you needn't bother to ascertain. I ascertained. They're real.'

'The books?'

He nodded.

'Absolutely real – have pages and everything. I thought they'd be a nice durable cardboard. Matter of fact, they're absolutely real. Pages and – Here! Lemme show you.'

Taking our scepticism for granted he rushed to the bookcase and returned with Volume One of the *Stoddard Lectures*.

'See!' he cried triumphantly. 'It's a bona fide piece of printed matter. It fooled me. This fella's a regular Belasco. It's a triumph. What thoroughness! What realism! Knew when to stop, too – didn't cut the pages. But what do you want? What do you expect?'

This extract reproduces many of the characteristic features of the first passage, the omission of grammatical elements, the repetition, and the abrupt breaking off of sentences, but behind it all one can detect the controlling hand of the novelist selecting and arranging to create the precise effect he wants. Besides suggesting the slight confusion in the drunk's speech, Fitzgerald lets us feel his mixture of amused condescension and contempt for Gatsby's phoney culture in the drunk's ironic admiration.

An even better illustration might be taken from Harold Pinter, a playwright with an acute ear for registering the speech rhythms of real life. His play, *The Caretaker*, begins with the following piece of dialogue:

ASTON: Sit down.

DAVIES: Thanks. (*Looking about*) Uuh. . . .

ASTON: Just a minute.

Aston looks around for a chair, sees one lying on its side by the rolled carpet at the fireplace, and starts to get it out.

DAVIES: Sit down? Huh. . . . I haven't had a good sit down. . . . I haven't had a good sit down . . . well, I couldn't tell you . . .

ASTON (*placing the chair*): Here you are.

DAVIES: Ten minutes off for tea-break in the middle of the night in that place and I couldn't find a seat, not one. All them Greeks had it. And they had me working there . . . they had me working. . . .

Aston sits on the bed, takes out a tobacco tin and papers, and begins to roll himself a cigarette. Davies watches him.

All them blacks had it. Blacks, Greeks, Poles the lot of them, that's what, doing me out of a seat, treating me like dirt. When he come at me tonight, I told him

This is naturalistic dialogue indeed! (Some critics claim that Pinter carries his naturalism to absurd lengths.) Behind the hesitations and the repetitions, however, there is a progression of ideas, and slowly and gradually the audience is being given its first glimpse into the character of the tramp Davies. The invitation to sit down lets loose the floodgates of his self-pity, his resentment at the way he is treated, and his racial prejudice. Behind the apparent incoherence there is a careful structuring of ideas.

In contrast to the genuine conversation, the literary extracts both reveal a conscious and deliberate shaping of the raw material of language into an artistic pattern which conveys some significance as well as meaning. Both are examples of spoken prose, prose being according to Professor Abercrombie's 'language organized for *visual* presentation'. A conversation cannot really be got down in ordinary writing since writing is a device specifically developed for recording prose, not conversation. One of the tasks of the actors in *The Caretaker* will be to superimpose appropriate intonation patterns upon the purely visual material they have in the printed texts.

Try examining all three passages for items of vocabulary, grammar, and syntax which are features of conversation but which would be inappropriate in formal prose.

2

The Varieties of Prose

As we have seen, there are any number of different varieties of prose, the differences in language and syntax reflecting to a large extent the different purposes of the writers. Every piece of writing is, of course, unique since no two people are exactly alike and their writing is the product of their individual characteristics. When the personal element is accounted for, however, most varieties of prose will be found to have a substratum of language common to all of them, which is determined largely by the purpose behind the prose. Before we go on to consider this, however, we ought to reflect for a moment on the *basic* purposes for which we use language.

THE PRINCIPAL USES OF LANGUAGE

Broadly speaking, in terms of purpose we can use language in three ways – *informatively*, *expressively*, and *directively*.

(i) We use language *informatively* when we are communicating information, describing the world around us and reasoning about it. When we write a report of some event or an account of some process or try to transmit ideas to other people, we are using language in this way. Scientific reports or descriptions are perhaps the purest examples of prose of this kind. For example:

Calcium, atomic number 20 (symbol Ca, atomic weight 40.1) is a metal belonging, together with strontium, barium, and radium, to the class known as alkaline – earth metals, on account of the alkalinity of their oxides. The carbonate occurs as limestone, coral, marble and calcspar (calcite).

(ii) We use language *expressively* when our purpose is not to convey facts about the world but to impart feelings, emotions, or attitudes. Although poetry provides us with the expressive use of language in its most concentrated form, we all use language in this way in our everyday lives. We express sympathy and sorrow by using phrases such as 'How sad!' or 'How sorry I am!', we betray our excitement and enthusiasm by shouts and exclamations of all kinds, and demonstrate love and affection by all kinds of endearments. In every case we are using language expressively to convey our feelings and attitudes.

There are two aspects of the expressive use of language: we can be using language to express our own feelings and at the same time to arouse similar feelings in others. We both evince and evoke feelings. For example:

> The next thing I remember is, waking up with a feeling as if I had had a frightful nightmare, and seeing before me a terrible red glare, crossed with thick black bars. I heard voices, too, speaking with a hollow sound, and as if muffled by a rush of wind or water: agitation, uncertainty, and an all predominating sense of terror confused my faculties.

CHARLOTTE BRONTË, *Jane Eyre*

(iii) Finally, we use language *directively* when we use it to cause (or prevent) action, for instance when we use it to make somebody do something. Obviously the clearest examples of the directive use of language are commands and requests. Questions also come into this category because when we ask a question, we expect an answer. Recipes are directive language in almost pure form. For example:

> Pour the stew into a casserole dish. Put a lid on the dish. Put the dish in the centre of the preheated oven for 20 mins. At the same time, mix the flour with a pinch of salt and the baking powder in a bowl. Rub in the margarine until the mixture looks like fine bread-crumbs. Add enough of the beaten egg to make a soft dough.

Now, clearly, in most writing these three basic uses of language are not kept rigidly separate. Sometimes all three will appear in the same piece of prose. A sermon, the purpose of which is primarily directive since it seeks to encourage a certain type of conduct, will almost certainly use language expressively also, since it is very difficult to persuade people to do something simply by appealing to their rational intellects. Few people are roused to action unless their emotions are stirred (a simple psychological fact which Brutus failed to grasp in addressing the populace in *Julius Caesar*. Mark Antony made no such mistake).

Unfortunately for our purposes, there is no direct connection between the grammatical form of a sentence and the purpose for which it is being used. Sentences can be classified grammatically as statements, questions, commands, and exclamations. It would be delightfully simple and convenient if every time we used language informatively we used the statement form, a question or command when using language directively, and an exclamation for expressive purposes.

But this is not how language operates. The guest who says to his hostess, 'I have had a delightful evening', is using a declarative sentence for an expressive purpose – to inform his hostess of his feelings (real or feigned) of gratitude and appreciation. Similarly, since a direct command outside the armed services often seems brusque and ill-mannered, a declarative sentence is sometimes used when the purpose is directive. It would be a very stupid employee indeed who regarded his employer's statement, 'I should like to see you in my room at four o'clock', as simply a remark conveying information about his boss's state of mind. Or again, a young lady walking with her boy-friend who exclaims, 'Oh! What a lovely moon!' uses expressive language but her basic purpose may well be to initiate action. In every case, therefore, it is necessary to interpret the situation in the light of the context to determine how the language is being used.

PROSE AND PURPOSE

As we have seen, the English language is not a single thing but consists of a whole host of different varieties which we lump under the term English. One of the first things we must do, therefore, in the close reading of any passage of prose is to decide what *kind* of prose it is. These different kinds of English are all more or less independent and have a number of characteristics in sound, grammar, and vocabulary which allow us to differentiate between them. By examining specific features of grammar and vocabulary we can place a piece of prose in its appropriate broad category.

Just as the purpose for which it was written shapes the features of the prose in broad categories of writing, so the kind of prose that comes to be written within a category, or within a single work, is determined by a complex combination of factors; for all prose writers approach their task under certain conditions that affect what they write. When we look at a stretch of prose for practical criticism we should not only identify the category, but be aware of the factors which have operated to produce the particular language variety.

THE PURPOSE BEHIND THE WRITING

If a writer's purpose is to transmit knowledge in a particular field of study his prose will be different from that of a writer in another field whose aim is to inculcate a point of view. The two writers will deploy their language in different ways to suit their different aims. Compare these two short extracts. The first is a piece of fairly popular scientific exposition, the second a piece of popular journalism:

Out of the total range of audibly distinct sounds a human being can produce (a very large number indeed) only a limited number are used in any one language.

Bewitched, Battered and Bewildered.
Such is the state of the Labour Party this morning.

Even these very brief quotations reflect the differing aims behind the prose. But even within a category there can be language variations: a popular scientific book will require at least a different vocabulary from one written for specialists, and a work of fiction intended for children will clearly need to be different in some respects from one written for adults.

THE SITUATION OF THE WRITER

Linguists, those who study language as language, see it as a form of social behaviour, and since society divides into different social groups of one kind or another, language reflects these different social groupings.

The most obvious social grouping is one brought about by *geographical* conditions. We live in different parts of these islands, or of the world, and people in one place tend to speak and write English in a different way from people in another place. These differences reveal themselves in two distinct ways: if they involve differences in patterns of grammar and vocabulary, we are concerned with different *dialects* of English. If the grammar and vocabulary is more or less the same as the standard forms and only the sound pattern, i.e. the pronunciation, varies then we are concerned with *accents*. The problem of dialect and its use is illuminated by this extract from Lewis Grassic Gibbon's *Sunset Song* which is set in the county of Kincardine in Scotland:

Up at Rob's table an argument rose, Chris hoped that it wasn't religion, she saw Mr Gordon's wee face pecked up to counter Rob. But Rob was just saying what a shame it was that folk should be shamed nowadays to speak Scotch – or they called it Scots if they did, the split-tongued sourocks! Every damned little narrow-dowped rat that you met put on the English if he thought he'd impress you – as though Scotch wasn't good enough now, it had words in it that the thin bit of scraichs of the English could never come at. And Rob said *You can tell me, man, what's the English for sotter, or greip, or smore, or pleiter, gloaming or glunching or well-kenspeckled? And if you said gloaming was sunset you'd fair be a liar; and you're hardly that, Mr Gordon.*

But Gordon was real decent and reasonable, *You can't help it, Rob. If folk are to get on in the world nowadays away from the ploughshafts and out of the pleiter, they must use the English, orra though it be.*

The differences in this passage from Standard English are mainly in vocabulary but there are variations in grammatical usage too. Apart from the obvious dialect forms, notice that words like 'real' and 'folk' are used in a different sense from the Standard usage. Rob's resentment at the decline of 'Scotch' (Scots) from an independent national language to a northern dialect of English is understandable, but the minister, Mr Gordon, feels that the process has gone too far to be reversible. It is worth noticing too that the author himself uses as his medium a form of Standard English laced with enough Scottish words and idioms and syntactical patterns to give it the flavour of Scottish speech.

It would be a mistake, however, to suggest that the language of Scotland is homogeneous. Many of the words Rob cites belong to the north-east corner of Scotland and would not be found uniformly over the rest of the country. Similarly, there are innumerable dialects in England. Here is D. H. Lawrence's attempt to reproduce the dialect of his native Nottinghamshire in *Sons and Lovers*. Walter Morel, a miner, is describing an encounter with the mine manager.

Th' gaffer come down to our stall this morning, an' 'e says, 'You know, Walter this 'ere'll not do. What about these props?' 'It'll never do this 'ere,' 'e says. 'You'll be havin' the roof in, one o' these days.'

An' I says, 'Tha'd better stan' on a bit o' clunch then, an' hold it up wi' thy 'edd.' So 'e wor that mad, 'e cossed an' 'e swore, an' t'other chaps they did laugh.'

A good many of the typographical peculiarities of this passage stem from Lawrence's attempt to suggest the pronunciation, the sound patterns of the dialect, particularly the elision of initial and final consonants and vowels, but there are distinctive lexical and grammatical variations from the standard variety of English also. Note particularly the dialect's retention of the archaic form of the second person pronoun in 'Tha' and 'thy', forms which in modern Standard English are almost entirely confined to religious language. Note too how 'wor' (or 'were') replaces the normal 'was' of the third person singular past tense, and that the past tense of the verb 'to come' remains 'come'. Try to identify some more of the devices which Lawrence used to confer authenticity.

Our language then frequently reflects where we come from; it changes in terms of place. The second social grouping it reflects is that based on *social and educational level*. Within a particular community the language of groups of roughly similar economic status or similar educational attainments will tend to show characteristics which differentiate it from the language of groups with different incomes and patterns of education. Working-class language reveals markedly different patterns from middle-class language, and there are subtle nuances between the latter and upper-middle-class and aristocratic usage.

The nature and the importance of these variations is trenchantly illustrated by this extract from the *New Statesman* of 23 July 1971, in an article describing the effects of long-term unemployment on the working population of the north of England. An unemployed fitter had made himself spokesman for his less articulate mates at the Department of Social Security, although he himself, according to the writer of the article, was 'barely literate'. He was shrewd enough, however, to realize the importance of language in this delicate situation:

> I learnt the language, see. If we ask, 'D'ya give owt for bairns?' we get nowt. If I march in respectful and say, 'Do the children qualify for an exceptional needs grant?' – it bloody works.

In our reading, however, we are most likely to come across language revealing regional or class characteristics in passages of dialogue within novels or plays, although some novelists using first person narrators have chosen to present their stories in the vernacular. The most famous example is probably Mark Twain's *Huckleberry Finn* and a modern instance would be J. D. Salinger's *The Catcher in the Rye* which uses the racy, urban colloquial speech of a middle-class New York teenager.

FACTORS BEHIND PROSE WRITING

Normally the passages of prose we are required to assess are not deviant forms of English but will be written in the standard forms of the language. Nevertheless they will vary one from another, and we must now turn to a consideration of the factors which determine the variations so that we can decide what kind of prose we are dealing with in each case. The writer of prose may be concerned with a number of specific tasks: the communication of ideas, the reporting of facts, the inculcation of beliefs, the evoking of attitudes, the correction of abuses, the enlightenment or entertainment of his readers, and so on.

His medium is the half a million or so words of the English language, an instrument of vast range and infinite flexibility. At first sight he would seem to have almost unlimited choice of vocabulary in a language rich in synonyms from which he can select to obtain the utmost precision or subtlety of meaning, the maximum of suggestiveness or colour. He has also at his command a number of basic grammatical structures which can be almost infinitely varied and combined to achieve the exact emphasis or arrangement he desires. In practice, however, his freedom is restricted, for the selection he can make within these two areas is determined by a number of factors.

(a) *Subject Matter*

In the first place the selection will obviously be affected by the nature of the *subject matter* the writer is dealing with. The writer of a scientific textbook will necessarily require to draw upon a fund of technical scientific terms; a law reporter is likely to use a considerable number of legal terms; and so on. The kinds of grammatical structure appropriate to these particular fields will also be limited. Thus the content of the writing will limit the range of choice open to the writer.

(b) *Purpose*

Secondly, how the writer deploys the techniques of vocabulary and grammar available to him will be determined to a very large extent by his *purpose* in writing. The language suitable for explaining the principles behind the internal combustion engine is not at all adapted to relating a passionate personal experience; the language of a formal report of a municipal council meeting is not characteristic of the language used in an informal letter to a friend. The writer's intention may be merely to provide information as in a textbook; it may be to convert the reader to a point of view as in a thesis, a polemical work, an editorial, or a political speech; it may be to lead us into a fictional world which, until written, exists only in the mind of an author. Whatever the purpose, it will be reflected in the choice of vocabulary and syntactical patterns.

(c) *The Audience*

Thirdly, the writer of prose must take into consideration the *audience* he is aiming at. A writer writes *for* somebody, or *for* a class of people. The language of the 'quality' daily and Sunday newspapers, which have a relatively restricted but fairly well-educated readership drawn mainly from the middle and professional classes, is very different from the language employed in the more popular newspapers with their mass circulations. Similarly, writers aiming at a children's audience must take care to employ language and grammatical structures simple enough for the readers to comprehend but without giving the impression of writing down.

(d) *Personal*

Fourthly, language reflects the differences between people, the *personal factor*. Every individual is biologically and genetically, physically, mentally and emotionally unique, and no two people use the resources of their native tongue exactly alike. Each person has an idiosyncratic way of selecting and arranging the linguistic material available to him. Indeed it has even been claimed that one writer's work can be distinguished from another's purely mechanically by using a computer to assess the proportions of certain linguistic forms which appear in their prose. In the practical criticism of prose we shall be particularly concerned, of course, with the unique individual effects achieved by the writer, not the mathematically computable aspects, which are of more use in providing evidence for authenticating disputed manuscripts.

(e) *Tone*

The last factor we shall consider is *tone*. In many kinds of prose writing the author can choose the tone he will adopt. Since, however, this is in itself determined by a combination of the writer's attitude to his material and his attitude to his audience and involves attention to subtleties of meaning, we will defer fuller consideration of this factor to a later chapter.

SOME EXAMPLES OF SPECIALIZED PROSE

We are now in a position to look at some examples of specialized uses of English and to isolate some of the most characteristic linguistic features which mark them off from one another. Basically, kinds of English vary in three ways: their sound patterns, their grammatical patterns, and their lexis or vocabulary.

Specialized sound patterns are most commonly found in language varieties intended to be spoken rather than written and we can therefore ignore most of them although we will be examining later some examples of oratory. To grasp what we mean by specialized sound patterns, however, think of the particularly oily and unctuous tones used in TV advertisements for food, the heartiness of the beer commercials, the bright, flippant chatter of disc jockeys, and the exaggeratedly excited, sometimes nearly hysterical, tones of many sports commentators.

Many specialized varieties of English can be easily recognized simply by noting the vocabulary used. From the large number of technical terms it contains, the following short passage manifestly belongs to the category of scientific writing:

Fluorine was first prepared in 1886 by Henri Moissan (1852–1907). He prepared it by electrolyzing a solution of potassium hydrogen fluoride, KHF, in liquid anhydrous hydrogen fluoride in a platinum tube, using platinum-iridium electrodes. Today it is prepared by electrolyzing a mixture of potassium fluoride and hydrogen fluoride in a stainless steel or copper electrolytic cell with a graphite anode.

Unless one has studied science and is familiar with the technical terms, the passage means very little. If one *is* conversant with the meaning of the scientific terms, then one can make even finer distinctions and identify the language of chemistry. Although the vocabulary is the most prominent feature there are some typical grammatical features as well. Two of the three sentences have verbs in the passive voice, for example, and a high percentage of verbs in the passive voice is one of the distinctive characteristics of scientific prose. This helps to give it the impersonal objectivity which is one of the goals of the scientific writer. The language is obviously being used informatively to transmit facts.

This passage patently deals with a very different area of experience:

The style of this poem, which Yeats wrote in October 1918, was still inadequate. For the second stanza read as sentimental hyperbole, and the contrast between the first and third stanzas was ineptly arranged. Except for 'crumbling', the adjectives were undistinguished and were, in the choice of 'star-laden', trite.

The vocabulary alone would suffice to allow us to identify what kind of writing this is. The cluster of nouns – 'style', 'poem', 'stanza', 'hyperbole', 'adjectives' – and the cluster of evaluative words and phrases – 'inadequate', 'sentimental', 'ineptly arranged', 'undistinguished', 'trite' – point straight to the area of literary criticism.

Both of these passages are clearly aimed at a fairly well-educated and sophisticated audience and certainly a minority audience with specialized interests. The next passage, however, is obviously designed to appeal to a much wider spectrum of the public:

> Renny Lister, pretty blonde actress, wife of actor Kenneth Cope, was at home in London, surrounded by her three energetic and vociferous children, happy to talk about anything – from her part in this week's episode of *Dixon of Dock Green* (Saturday 7.0 BBC1) to star signs of the zodiac. 'I'm Gemini, and they're quite nice people really. The kind that like to say "Let's have a party". I find astrology really can help. It makes me much more tolerant of other people because I understand their zodiac characteristics.' Her husband is Aries: 'You have to let Aries men think they're the boss.'

The chatty, gossipy style of this passage marks it off clearly as popular journalism. As such it shares certain grammatical features of this kind of writing which we will be examining later.

Distinctive grammatical features of varieties of prose are much more difficult to detect than the purely lexical ones, except where certain grammatical elements are omitted as is often the case in highly specialized forms of prose such as telegrams or newspaper headlines (for the sake of economy in either money or space), or in advertising English which has a fondness for sentences without verbs.

The elements omitted are usually minor parts of speech, one of whose functions in the sentence is to indicate what parts of speech the words they qualify belong to. Since many words in English can operate as more than one part of speech, the omission of these function indicators can sometimes lead to ludicrous ambiguities. Newspapers have been guilty of the following headlines among others: 'Giant Waves Down Queen Mary's Funnel' and 'McArthur Flies Back to Front'.

Professor Randolph Quirk in his invaluable book *The Use of English* has pointed out that a feature of much of the English of industry and commerce is the use of heavily pre-modified nominal groups – a group of words where a noun is modified by a large number of other words, demonstratives, adjectives, nouns and so on, all coming before it. Two examples he quotes are 'the Company's eight fixed open-hearth steel melting furnaces' and 'bovine submaxillary gland mucin'. As he points out, the latter group might well be rewritten as 'mucin from the submaxillary gland of cattle'; here the modifiers have been placed behind the noun which is the head word of the group. The disadvantage of the rearrangement is that the group has been increased in size from four to seven words; the advantage is that the meaning is perhaps more comprehensible to the layman.

A similar process might be applied to the first nominal group but the situation is not so simple in this instance since 'eight' must come before 'furnaces', this being the obligatory position for the numeral in English, with occasional literary exceptions like 'Soldiers Three' or 'fiddlers three' and phrases like 'Chapter One' or 'Book Two'. The group might then become 'eight furnaces of a fixed type with open hearth, for the melting of steel, belonging to the Company'. This heavy post-modification, however, is still clumsy, and perhaps a more balanced group would be preferable by distributing the modifiers before and after the head word giving 'the Company's eight furnaces of a fixed type with open hearths for the melting of steel'. Which version is the most satisfactory (and other variations are possible) is simply a matter of taste; but the example is an illustration of how much stylistic choice is open to a writer even in the elementary problem of composing a nominal group in a piece of technical prose.

Professor Quirk also highlights another area where there is a tendency for writers to modify nouns rather heavily – popular journalism. This tendency to pile up adjectives he illustrates with the quotation, 'this dark, slimly built young chemistry student', and he goes on to point out that where this heavy qualification is applied to the subject of a sentence it leads to a sentence rhythm which is not typical of English structure – 'Her 35-year-old Etonian husband, grandson of a millionaire, said . . .' It is more usual in English to place the heavily modified nouns after the verb as object or complement. Hence there arises another feature of certain varieties of journalistic style – a tendency to invert the normal order of the grammatical elements in the English sentence. This order is normally Subject, Predicator, Complement (including objects) and Adjuncts (modifying adverbial elements). Quirk quotes by way of illustration a paragraph in the *Daily Mail* of July 1958 beginning 'Said the new owner, 31-year-old Mrs Sheena Simmons, wife of a retired auctioneer from Bourne End. . . .' Here the positions of Subject and Predicate have been reversed.

We have touched on only a few aspects of the significance of the grammatical ordering of prose, a topic which will be handled in more detail in a later chapter. We hope, however, that we have provided sufficient evidence of the fact that the different varieties of English have characteristic lexical and grammatical features which are the basis of our recognition of them as separate kinds.

Exercises

Examine the following prose passages and try to determine the *kind* of prose they belong to. Consider such questions as, what type of periodical or book they are likely to have come from, what sort of audience they are aimed at, and what appears to be the writer's purpose. Justify your answers by specific references to vocabulary and grammatical forms where possible.

1. More years ago than I can bother to add up I was taking a walk through a forest of birches in north-eastern Germany, in Silesia to be exact. I was teaching English in a school in a small country town and walking with me on this afternoon was a wiry boy with a stoop and a damp nose, and spiky hair and glasses so thick that coming on him today in a thicket by the light of the full moon you'd think he was an invader from Mars slouching in incognito. Roughly you could say he was an intellectual or working up to one. He had a fierce dogmatic manner and a steady gleam in his eye. I didn't know him well but I respected his seriousness and his sincerity. Unhappily he was a disciple of an Austrian who was being much talked about, who was also serious and sincere and up to no good. The master's name was Adolf Hitler.

2. Already we must accept the fact that although we may discover contrasting themes and sections, and a large scale use of related or unrelated tonal areas, it would be foolish to expect sonata behaviour. In fact the first movement is one of the few individual Bruckner designs that is more or less describable by simple terminology, and it will save great confusion if we notice that the whole movement divides into two main sections (which we can label Statement and Counter-statement) with a huge but simple *coda* added.

3. When a rigid body is completely isolated so that no external forces act on it, clearly any velocity of translation, which the centre of mass

may have initially, is maintained indefinitely. This result is consonant with the principle of conservation of linear momentum which we have already discussed. Also the sum of the moments of the external forces about any axis through the centre of mass of the body is obviously zero. In that case the angular acccleration of the body about such an axis is zero and, therefore, the corresponding angular velocity is constant.

4. Once upon a time, very long ago, there was little Prince Ivan who was dumb. Never a word had he spoken from the day that he was born – not so much as a 'Yes' or a 'No', or a 'Please' or a 'Thank you'. A great sorrow he was to his father because he could not speak. indeed, neither his father nor his mother could bear the sight of him, for they thought, 'A poor sort of Tzar will a dumb boy make!' They even prayed, and said, 'If only we could have another child, whatever it is like, it could be no worse than this tongue-tied brat who cannot say a word.' And for that wish they were punished, as you shall hear.

5. Steering, serenely, his sutured brow, the sum of those several thrusting curves which seemed not of themselves to exert strength but merely to drink and send backward through them the energies of the guiding head they guided, a snake more splendid than Richard had ever seen before was just achieving a sandstone ledge and the first heat of the risen sun. In every wheaten scale and in all his barbaric patterning he was new and clear as gems, so gallant and sporting against the dun, he dazzled, and seeing him, Richard was acutely aware how sensitive, proud and tired he must be in his whole body, for it was clear that he had just struggled out of his old skin and was with his first return of strength venturing his new one.

6. When materialists try to defend the idea that living systems are nothing but machines they generally begin with the most automatic and involuntary activities they can think of. Those are the reflexes and instincts. Exactly what an instinct is has been the focus of much argument. Some people see the term to mean all the driving desires and passions of the flesh; others mean any reaction an organism is born with and so does not need to learn; and still others take the position that an instinct is any highly automatic involuntary sequence of responses.

7. One Messerschmitt went down in a sheet of flame on my right, and a Spitfire hurtled past in a half-roll; I was weaving and turning in a desperate attempt to gain height, with the machine practically hanging on the airscrew. Then, just below me and to my left, I saw what I had been praying for – a Messerschmitt climbing and away from the sun. I closed in to 200 yards, and from slightly to one side gave him a two-second burst: fabric ripped off the wing and black smoke poured from the engine, but he did not go down. Like a fool, I did not break away, but put in another three-second burst. Red flames shot upwards and he spiralled out of sight. At that moment, I felt a terrific explosion which knocked the control stick from my hand, and the whole machine quivered like a stricken animal.

3
The Element of Sound

. . . for he told of the long dead beasts of the Scottish land in the times when jungle flowered its forest across the Howe and a red sun rose on the steaming earth that the feet of man had still to tread; and he pictured the dark, slow tribes that came drifting across the low lands of the northern seas, the great bear watched them come and they hunted and fished and loved and died, God's children in the morn of time. . . .

LEWIS GRASSIC GIBBON, *Sunset Song*

I knew it. I knew if I came to this dinner, I'd draw something like this baby on my left. They've been saving him up for me for weeks. Now we've simply got to have him. . . .

DOROTHY PARKER, *But the One on the Right*

She trembled. Coming for her! There was no escape, no peace, no hope. She looked round despairingly. Suddenly the whole shadowy coast, the blurred islets, the heaven itself, swayed about twice, then came to rest. She closed her eyes and shouted.

JOSEPH CONRAD, *The Idiots*

If we have any ear for sound and rhythm at all it will be immediately apparent to us that the above three quotations differ markedly from each other, and that something of their total meaning comes from the particular way in which we 'hear' the words as we read. In the first passage there is a recurring regularity of certain rhythms; on three occasions there are three stressed words occurring together which provide a base from which the author develops further ideas in a long flow. These qualities of sound suggest something of the great historical movements of the past. In the second the irregularity of rhythm, combined with the monosyllables, reinforces the effect of flippant exasperation. In the third, something of the sense of panic is conveyed

24

by the short units into which the prose is divided and by the clever placing of strong stress throughout.

Nevertheless, however fascinating it may be to examine prose very closely for the sound element, and although the prose writer has to hand almost all of the sound devices available to the poet, the contribution of the sheer sound of words in prose is in general much less pronounced than in poetry, if only because the prose writer is usually more concerned with the clarity of his ideas and the coherence of their presentation. In general the more 'scientific' the prose the less will the sound matter; the more imaginative the prose the more is the writer likely to take care that the prose 'sounds' right for his purpose.

Sometimes differences in the placing of the stress can make for slight changes in significance. For example, did Lincoln in his speech at Gettysburg (which, incidentally, only one reporter thought worth recording) stress the prepositions or the noun in that celebrated sentence? Did he say:

> . . . that government *of* the people, *for* the people, *by* the people shall not perish from the earth,

or

> . . . that government of the *people*, for the *people*, by the *people* shall not perish from the earth.

So also with a sentence from Iris Murdoch's *Under the Net*:

> I looked at the house with suspicious curiosity and it seemed to be looking back at me.

Should we read this stressing 'it' and 'me' and, if so, why, and what difference does it make?

Most good writers are aware that prose is a clumsy and inefficient instrument for conveying by niceties of sound the precise meaning intended, or the kind of feeling the reader should experience in the reading. One crude method is the use of italics to indicate the strong stress of the speaking voice. The composer, Arthur Schoenberg, insisted in a letter to a friend:

> I can't say it often enough: my words are twelve-tone *compositions*, not *twelve-tone* compositions

and De Quincey in *The Bore at Chester* is reduced to:

> The idea pulled me up. *Not spoken to her?* Then I *would* speak to her. . . .

Lewis Grassic Gibbon tries, as many other writers have done, to convey something of the quality of sound by altering the spelling. In this particular instance it is the very broad Scottish vowels of one of the characters in *Sunset Song*:

> More like the head of one of Chrissie's faaaaaaaather's pigs, than a heraaaaaaaaaaldic animal, I'm afraaaaaaaaaaaaaaaaid.

While the subtler uses of sound are often difficult to estimate in prose, we should be on the look-out for instances in which meaning is reinforced or additional power given by alliteration, as happens, for example, in Dickens's 'bat in blisters, ball scorched brown' or in Joseph Heller's *Catch 22*, 'Men went mad and were rewarded with medals', or in Gibbon on the Oxford/Cambridge quarrel '. . . a question which has kindled such fierce and foolish disputes among their fanatic sons'.

There are, of course, occasions when the prose writer is directly describing sounds of various kinds and here the control of echoic or onomatopoetic effects can be a great asset. Thomas Hardy was a writer with an acute and discriminating ear for the sounds of nature, and his novels are full of passages describing the sound effects of the wind on vegetation and trees of various kinds. Where the average person would hear nothing but an undifferentiated buzz, Hardy could distinguish the individual notes making up the total harmony. He begins his novel *Under the Greenwood Tree* thus:

> To dwellers in a wood, almost every species of tree has its voice as well as its feature. At the passing of the breeze, the fir trees sob and moan no less distinctly than they rock; the holly whistles as it battles with itself; the ash hisses amid its quiverings; the beech rustles while its flat boughs rise and fall.

Here Hardy is exploiting the sound of individual words in 'sob', 'moan', 'whistle', 'hiss', and 'rustle' to suggest the differing tones the wind produces. It is also noticeable that there is a high proportion of sibilants (s, z, and sh sounds) in the whole passage. (Incidentally, as examples of Hardy's eye for movement as well, the verbs used to describe the motion of the different trees are worth looking at.) Hardy is deliberately appealing to our aural sense, and hence there is a minimum appeal to the visual imagination. Words which might conjure up visual images are left starkly unmodified, 'fir', 'holly', 'oak', 'beech'.

Joseph Conrad, describing a storm at sea in *The Nigger of the Nar-*

cissus, exhibits the same power to exploit the sounds of words to good effect:

> Outside the night moaned and sobbed to the accompaniment of a continuous loud tremor as of innumerable drums beating far off. Shrieks passed through the air. Tremendous dull blows made the ship tremble while she rolled under the weight of the seas toppling on deck. At times she soared up swiftly as if to leave this earth for ever, then during interminable moments fell through a void with all the hearts on board of her standing still, till a frightful shock, expected and sudden, started them off again with a big thump.

Apart from the directly echoic words like 'drums' and 'thump' in this passage, the most interesting feature is the way in which the shuddering of the ship is suggested by the repetition of the *tre* sound in 'tremor', 'tremendous', and 'tremble' along with the high proportion of *n* and *l* sounds. Notice, too, how both Hardy and Conrad use 'sob' and 'moan' for the sound of the wind through the trees and the rigging respectively.

THE RHYTHM OF PROSE

The last two short extracts from novels illustrate the direct exploitation of the sound values of words. It is difficult to analyse the rhythms of prose in any clear-cut meaningful way since they are very seldom as regular as the rhythms of poetry. We are unlikely to meet with many flights of fancy such as we find in Charles Lamb's essay *South Sea House* where he introduced two virtual pentameters, 'Dusty maps of Mexico, dim as dreams, and soundings in the bay of Panama'. But we can come to notice how the rhythm of a passage may be arranged so that it complements the idea or the emotion expressed by the words. The opening of Gibbon's *Autobiography* has an urbane, confident, relaxed rhythm:

> In the fifty-second year of my age, after the completion of a toilsome and successful work, I now propose to employ some moments of my leisure in reviewing the simple transactions of a private and literary life.

Notice, too, that the past and the future are linked by three words in a central position in the sentence and all carry stress – 'I now propose'. Similarly we can sense a rhythmic pattern in the dying fall of the next two passages, the first the concluding paragraph of Hardy's

Tess of the D'Urbervilles and the second the description of George Osborne's death in Thackeray's *Vanity Fair*:

Justice was done, and the President of the Immortals, in Aeschylean phrase, had ended his sport with Tess. And the d'Urberville knights and dames slept on in their tombs unknowing. The two speechless gazers bent themselves down to the earth, as if in prayer, and remained thus a long time, absolutely motionless: the flag continued to wave silently. As soon as they had strength they arose, joined hands again, and went on.

No more firing was heard at Brussels – the pursuit rolled miles away. Darkness came down on the field and city; and Amelia was praying for George, who was lying on his face, dead, with a bullet through his heart.

The precise sound basis of the rhythms of these passages is extremely difficult to pin down. It is not a matter of *regular* patterns of stressed and unstressed syllables, although these must contribute something to the total effect. Rather it is a question of the arrangement of phrases (in the musical not the grammatical sense of the term) and the distribution of pauses within the sentence. It is noticeable that the first sentence of the Hardy passage consists of four phrases and consequently three pauses. This pattern is repeated in sentences three and four, the lengths of the phrases varying in length. The third sentence, of course, has an additional clause after the colon but this parallels the simpler phrasal structure of the second sentence. Thus the complex rhythmical structure of the paragraph appears to be made up of three sentences constructed of four phrases, with two single-phrase sentences separating them.

The importance of length of phrase and pause is even more marked in the Thackeray extract, particularly in the last sentence with the isolation of the word 'dead'. (Try placing it in different positions and noting the difference in rhythm.)

It is significant that both passages are attempts to portray the pathos of death (Tess has just been hanged for murder) and are written under the stress of heightened emotion. The poet George Barker, in a radio talk on the 'prose poem' reproduced in *The Listener* of 10 June 1971, gave this account of the creative process behind this phenomenon:

I think that what happens when prose approaches the condition of poetry is something like this: contemplating a given object or subject, the susceptibilities of the writer are brought into a state of heightened excitement, as, for instance, when Dickens described the death of Little Nell. You'll remember that, ever afterwards, when he read this passage in public, he finished up in tears. This description is written in a prose undistinguishable from blank verse. Such excitement could, I think be called an elation or inspiration of mind and this excitement tends quite naturally and instinctively to express itself, it relieves itself in recurring rhythms, much as the body in the dance.

THE RHYTHMS OF ORATORY

This tendency for emotional prose to become rhythmical can frequently be seen in oratory, for in a speech the speaker is frequently aiming partly at the feelings of his audience. The rhythm and cadence of the sentences therefore play an important role in the total effect, particularly at the end, the climax or peroration.

Abraham Lincoln's rightly famous Dedicatory Address at the Gettysburg Cemetery during the American Civil War illustrates well the use of controlled rhythms in prose:

Fourscore and seven years ago our fathers brought forth upon this continent a new nation, conceived in liberty, and dedicated to the proposition that all men are created equal. Now we are engaged in a great Civil War, testing whether that nation, or any nation so conceived and so dedicated, can long endure. We are met on a great battlefield of that war. We have come to dedicate a portion of that field as a final resting place of those who gave their lives that the nation might live. It is altogether fitting that we should do this. But in a larger sense we cannot dedicate, we cannot consecrate, we cannot hallow this ground. The brave men living and dead, who struggled here, have consecrated it far above our power to add or detract. The world will little note, nor long remember what we say here, but it can never forget what they did here. It is for us, the living, rather to be dedicated here to the unfinished work they have thus so far so nobly advanced. It is rather for us to be here dedicated to the great task remaining before us, that from these honoured dead we take increased devotion to that cause for which they gave the last full measure of devotion; that we here highly resolve that the dead shall not have died in vain, that the nation shall, under God, have a new birth of freedom, and that the government of the people, by the people, and for the people, shall not perish from the earth.

From the sentiments expressed, it is clear that Lincoln had a double purpose in delivering this speech. The ostensible one, of course, was to dedicate the cemetery at Gettsburg but he was also taking the opportunity to exhort his audience to pursue with renewed vigour the struggle against the South.

If we examine the speech carefully, we find that there is a very subtle interplay of sounds and rhythms. The passage opens with two fairly long sentences. These are followed by a number of shorter sentences of medium length which gradually lead on to the very long final sentence with its succession of noun clauses all introduced by 'that', rising to the final climax with its repeated parallel structures – 'government of the people, by the people, and for the people, shall not perish from the earth'.

There are a number of other features of the rhythmical structure of the passage. In the spoken word a certain amount of repetition is advisable since the message must be grasped by the ear alone. In the middle of the speech we find: 'But in a larger sense we cannot dedicate, we cannot consecrate, we cannot hallow this ground'. The repeated syntactical structures contain verbs which mean roughly the same thing. No new idea is introduced by the three clauses but the original idea is emphasized by reiteration. The next sentence but one with its balanced structure also adds its quota to the rhythmical effect of the whole speech. Note the corresponding balance of ideas in 'remember' and 'forget', 'what we say' and 'what they did'. (It is one of the ironies of history that the sentiments expressed here by Lincoln have not been confirmed by time. Many who have no idea what happened at Gettysburg are familiar, however vaguely, with the words Lincoln spoke on the battlefield. Such is the power of language used effectively.)

Finally, note how skilfully Lincoln repeats the verbs 'dedicate' and 'dedicated', usually in stressed positions so that they ring out like a series of hammer blows. The effect of this, along with the associated words like 'consecrate', 'hallow', and 'devotion' is to make the speech a call to the nation to take up some holy crusade.

There is, of course, a great deal more of stylistic interest in this passage which is worth looking at, some of which might be discussed under other headings. The parallel syntactical structures we have been looking at, for instance, really form part of the grammatical elements of the passage, but they contribute to the sound and the rhythm, and here that seems to be their principal function. Interesting grammatically is also the use of 'that' throughout the passage, at the beginning of the speech mainly as a demonstrative – 'that nation', 'that war', 'that battlefield', and later as a conjunction introducing a series of declarations of purpose and resolution. Worth considering, too, is the use of the first person plural 'we' throughout. (Compare the unfortunately worded war-time poster's use of pronouns: 'Your courage, your hard work, will give us victory'.) An equally famous piece of oratory which repays analysis of its rhythmical qualities is Burke's reference to Marie Antoinette from his *Reflections on the Revolution in France.* This is a very rhetorical piece in comparison with the more restrained emotion of Lincoln's address but the same techniques are employed.

It is now sixteen or seventeen years since I saw the queen of France, then the Dauphiness, at Versailles; and surely never lighted on this orb, which she hardly seemed to touch, a more delightful vision. I saw her just above the horizon, decorating and cheering the elevated sphere she just began to move in; glittering like the morning star, full of life, and splendour and joy. Oh what a revolution! and what a heart must I have, to contemplate without emotion that elevation and that fall! Little did I dream when she added titles of veneration to those of enthusiastic, distant, respectful love, that she should ever be obliged to carry the sharp antidote against disgrace concealed in that bosom; little did I dream that I should have lived to see such disasters fallen upon her in a nation of gallant men, in a nation of men of honour and cavaliers. I thought ten thousand swords must have leapt from their scabbards to avenge even a look that threatened her with insult. – But the age of chivalry is gone. That of sophisters, economists, and calculators has succeeded; and the glory of Europe is extinguished for ever. Never, never more, shall we behold that generous loyalty to rank and sex, that proud submission, that dignified obedience, that subordination of the heart, which kept alive, even in servitude itself, the spirit of an exalted freedom. The unbought grace of life, the cheap defence of nations, the nurse of manly sentiments and heroic enterprise, is gone! It is gone, that sensibility of principle, that chastity of honour, which felt a stain like a wound, which inspired courage whilst it mitigated ferocity, which ennobled whatever it touched, and under which vice itself lost half its wit, by losing all its grossness.

To get the full flavour of the cadences of this passage it must be read aloud. In analysing the rhythm it becomes clear that once again, as in the Lincoln speech, we must examine the syntactical patterns of the sentences, since the rhythmical cadences are built up out of the subtle repetition and variation of similar grammatical features.

The first sentence consists of two independent clauses divided by the semi-colon, and the intonation pattern of the first half of the sentence is paralleled by that of the second, the flow of the first clause being interrupted by the parenthetic phrase, 'then the Dauphiness', and that of the second clause by the parenthetic clause, 'which she hardly seemed to touch'. The second clause also has a inversion of Subject and Predicate. The second sentence, with its heavy modification of the object 'her' with repeated participles, follows the normal pattern of the English sentence but is followed by the two exclamatory sentences beginning with 'Oh, what a revolution . . .' and 'Little did I dream . . .' both of which have the inversion of Subject and Predicate characteristic of the exclamatory sentence. Notice too the effect obtained by placing the Adjunct 'without emotion' between the verb and the object so that the emphasis falls upon 'that elevation and that fall'. The phrase 'Little did I dream . . .' is repeated as an introduction to the second part of the sentence to provide a parallel structure.

After the sentence expressing his incredulity at the way Frenchmen had failed to rally to Marie Antoinette's defence, Burke breaks off to moralize on the decay of idealism with the short abrupt sentence, 'But the age of chivalry is gone!' and this is followed by the elegiac dying fall of the next sentence. Throughout the last three long sentences the phrase 'It is gone' re-echoes. The structures of the three sentences are subtly varied to provide a variety of rhythms. The first one beginning 'Never, never more . . .' has an inversion of Subject and Predicate and an extended Complement consisting of a number of noun phrases; the next sentence reverses that structure, piling up the noun phrase in the subject, which, as we have seen, is atypical in English, and ending with the simple Predicate 'is gone;' the final sentence then returns to the pattern of the first, allowing Burke to reiterate 'It is gone' and building up to a climax of adjective clauses.

The rhythm is, of course, only one of the elements which Burke uses to play upon the emotions of his audience. Just as important is the vocabulary he uses, the consideration of which should really be postponed until we examine the element of meaning. However, it is probably more convenient and more natural to anticipate the final chapter of the book and discuss the vocabulary now.

Notice first of all the extravagant terms Burke uses to introduce Marie Antoinette, and the image which lies behind his description of some ethereal celestial body rising above the horizon radiating majesty and splendour. The image is particularly apt since Marie Antoinette's rise to the zenith of her triumphal progress is followed by her fall. Notice also the emotive connotations of the words Burke uses to portray the qualities he associated with the shattered French feudal monarchical system – 'generous loyalty', 'proud submission', 'dignified obedience', 'subordination of the heart', 'exalted freedom', 'manly sentiments', 'heroic enterprise', etc., etc. Thus he selects the noble, heroic, and idealistic aspects of the system for the listener's approbation. There were, of course, more unsavoury aspects which he chose to ignore but which the French people regarded as important. Notice, too, how in the context the terms 'economists' and 'calculators', two fairly neutral words in most circumstances, take on such pejorative emotional connotations, with their suggestions of materialism and money-grubbing in contrast with the implied idealism of chivalry.

RHYTHM IN DISCURSIVE PROSE

Both Lincoln and Burke were using prose intended to be heard rather than read but the practice of Edward Gibbon, the author of *The Decline and Fall of the Roman Empire*, suggests that many great writers have been very self-conscious about the sound and rhythm of prose intended to be read and heard by the inner ear only. Gibbon took great pains with the rhythmical unity of his paragraphs. In his *Autobiography* he wrote:

It has always been my practice to cast a long paragraph in a single mould, to try it by my ear, to deposit it in my memory, but to suspend the action of the pen till I had given the last polish to my work.

This kind of very consciously shaped prose is perhaps not much in favour nowadays, for modern taste is in favour of something which gives less impression of conscious artistry. Nevertheless, the carefully modulated prose of Gibbon can be a very effective means of communication, as this excerpt, chosen at random from *The Decline and Fall of the Roman Empire*, illustrates:

The virtue of Marcus Aurelius Antoninus was of a severer and more laborious kind. It was the well-earned harvest of many a learned conference, and many a midnight lucubration. At the age of twelve years he embraced the rigid system of the Stoics which taught him to submit his body to his mind, his passion to his reason; to consider virtue as the only good, vice as the only evil, all things external as things indifferent. His *Meditations*, composed in the tumult of a camp, are still extant: and he even condescended to give lessons of philosophy, in a more public manner than was perhaps consistent with the modesty of a sage or the dignity of an emperor. But his life was the noblest commentary on the precepts of Zeno. He was severe to himself, indulgent to the imperfections of others, just and beneficent to all mankind. He regretted that Avidius Cassius, who excited a rebellion in Syria, had disappointed him, by a voluntary death, of the pleasure of converting an enemy into a friend; and he justified the sincerity of that sentiment by moderating the zeal of the senate against the adherents of the traitor. War he detested, as the disgrace and calamity of human nature, but when the necessity of a just defence called upon him to take up arms, he readily exposed his person to eight winter campaigns on the frozen banks of the Danube, the severity of which was at last fatal to the weakness of his constitution. His memory was revered by a grateful posterity, and above a century after his death, many persons preserved the image of Marcus Antoninus among those of their household gods.

A careful analysis of the rhythm of this paragraph shows it to be based principally on a simple variation of parallel structures, either double or triple, particularly in the first part of the paragraph. The first sentence has a double comparative, 'severer' and 'more laborious', the extended form of the latter providing variety. The second has the first triple structure – 'of many a learned conference, of many a patient lecture, and many a midnight lucubration'. In the next sentence the adjective clause qualifying 'Stoics' has a double complement to 'taught' – 'to submit . . . and 'to consider . . .' These complements are themselves subdivided, into two parallel structures in the first instance, and into three in the second, 'his body to his mind, his passions to his reason' and 'virtue as the only good, vice as the only evil, all things external as things indifferent'. The following sentence consists of two independent clauses and at the end we encounter the by now expected repetition, 'the modesty of a sage or the dignity of an emperor'.

(You might consider whether the double and triple structure is maintained throughout the rest of the paragraph.)

A further element in the pattern of sound and rhythm of the paragraph is the careful variation in the length and complexity of the sentences. The paragraph is carefully balanced, the first part devoted to the learning of Marcus Aurelius, the second to his life. Each part is introduced by a short sentence, followed by a longer one displaying the characteristic triple repetition. Thereafter the sentences increase in length in each section but retain a relatively simple structure. Only one clause shows any deviation from the normal pattern of the English sentence, 'War he detested', to place the stress on the first word.

The disadvantages of this kind of rather mannered prose are fairly obvious. While the paragraph does have a certain dignified flow, the reader may well feel that the introduction of the double and triple structures becomes a mechanical habit, that they become a rigid mould into which Gibbon's thoughts are poured whether they fit the nature of these ideas or not.

THE INTERDEPENDENCE OF THE BASIC ELEMENTS

This chapter is devoted to the element of sound in prose, yet throughout we have found ourselves compelled to refer constantly to grammatical structures, the subject matter of our next chapter. This illustrates in a practical way how much the elements we have abstracted for analytical purposes are in fact mutually dependent. In reality all three elements make their impact in concert, and the rather artificial separation simply makes for ease of description.

Exercises – Sound

Assess the contribution sound makes to the following passages:

1. He thought his happiness was complete when, as he meandered aimlessly along, suddenly he stood by the edge of a full-fed river. Never in his life had he seen a river before – this sleek, sinuous, full-bodied animal, chasing and chuckling, gripping things with a gurgle and leaving them with a laugh, to fling itself on fresh play-mates that shook themselves free, and were caught and held again. All was a-shake and a-shiver – glints and gleams and sparkles, rustle and swirl, chatter and bubble.

KENNETH GRAHAME, *The Wind in the Willows*

2. Rude brutal anger routed the last lingering instant of ecstasy from his soul. It broke up violently her fair image and flung the fragments on all sides. On all sides distorted reflections of her image started from his memory.

JAMES JOYCE, *Portrait of the Artist as a Young Man*

Analyse the rhythym of the following passages and try to suggest what contribution they make to the meaning:

3. The eighteenth century – 'the silver age of the European Renaissance' – virtually begins in the final decades of the seventeenth. When we enter those decades we recognize on all sides the familiar eighteenth-century landmarks, lit by the familiar illuminations of the time. Glory and loveliness may have passed away, but so also have the fogs and glooms of history; the common daylight which now descends upon a distracted world may be prosaic, but at least it is steady and serene, and has not yet become dark with excessive light. One meets everywhere a sense of relief and escape, relief from the strain of living in a mysterious universe, and escape from the barbarism of the Gothic centuries. Nature's laws had been explained by the New Philosophy; sanity, culture, and civilization had revived; and at last, across the vast gulf of the monkish and deluded past, one could salute the ancients from an eminence perhaps as lofty as their own.

BASIL WILLEY, The Eighteenth Century Background

4. The philosopher, who with calm suspicion examines the dreams and omens, the miracles and prodigies, of profane or even of ecclesiastical history, will probably conclude that, if the eyes of the spectators have sometimes been deceived by fraud, the understanding of the readers has much more frequently been insulted by fiction. Every event, or appearance, or accident, which seems to deviate from the ordinary course of nature, has been rashly ascribed to the immediate action of the Deity; and the astonished fancy of the multitude has sometimes given shape and colour, language and motion, to the fleeting but uncommon meteors of the air.

EDWARD GIBBON, The Decline and Fall of the Roman Empire

5. We have always thought it strange that, while the history of the Spanish Empire in America is familiarly known to all nations of Europe, the great actions of our countrymen in the East should, even among ourselves, excite little interest. Every schoolboy knows who imprisoned Montezuma, and who strangled Atahualpa. But we doubt whether one in ten, even among English gentlemen of highly cultivated minds, can tell who won the battle of Buxar, who perpetrated the massacre of Patna, whether Sujah Dowlah rules in Oude or Travancore, or whether Holko was a Hindoo or a Mussulman.

Yet the victories of Cortes were gained over savages who had no letters, who were ignorant of the use of metals, who had not broken in a single animal to labour, who wielded no better weapons than those which could be made out of sticks, flints, and fish-bones, who regarded a horse-soldier as a monster, half-man and half-beast, who took a harquebusier for a sorcerer, able to scatter the thunder and lightning of the skies. The people of India, when we subdued them, were ten times as numerous as the Americans whom the Spaniards vanquished, and were at the same time quite as highly civilized as the victorious Spaniards. They had reared cities larger and fairer than Saragossa or Toledo, and buildings more beautiful and costly than the cathedral of Seville. They could show bankers richer than the richest firms of Barcelona or Cadiz, viceroys whose splendour far surpassed that of Ferdinand the Catholic; myriads of cavalry and long trains of artillery which would have astonished the Great Captain.

MACAULAY, *Essay on Clive*

6. Even though large tracts of Europe and many old and famous states have fallen or may fall into the grip of the Gestapo and all the odious apparatus of Nazi rule, we shall not flag or fail. We shall fight in France, we shall fight in the seas and oceans, we shall fight with growing confidence and growing strength in the air; we shall defend our island, whatever the cost may be. We shall fight on the beaches, we shall fight on the landing-grounds, we shall fight in the fields and in the streets; we shall never surrender; and even if, which I do not for a moment believe, this Island or a large part of it were subjugated and starving, then our Empire beyond the seas, armed and guarded by the British Fleet, would carry on the struggle, until, in God's good time, the New World, with all its power and might, steps forth to the rescue and the liberation of the old.

WINSTON CHURCHILL, *Speech to Parliament 4 June 1940*

4

The Grammatical Element

The grammatical element in meaning has two components; first, the form of words and the classes they belong to, and second the way in which they are strung together to make sense (in grammatical terms 'morphology' and 'syntax'). Prose is likely to be much more regular than poetry in both these respects since the prose writer is normally granted much less freedom than the poet to distort the normal forms of language for purposes of expression.

WORD FORMS

Unusual word forms such as the compound coinages we find in a poet like Hopkins are, therefore, much rarer in prose than in poetry. However, new words are continually being coined as the need arises. Journalists, who often like to write what they think is a crisp and snappy style, sometimes coin new words by telescoping two words together to create a third with the connotations of both the originals. A 'shamateur' combines 'sham' and 'amateur' to designate a sportsman who has amateur status but in fact gains materially from playing or competing.

The commercial world gives us 'beefburger' from 'beef' and 'hamburger'. This is a particularly interesting example since the original word is derived from the real or imagined place of origin of this particular article of food. The derivative 'beefburger', however, suggests something quite different – that the word is a combination of 'ham' and 'burger'. This is therefore that kind of coinage which tends to provoke indignant letters to *The Times* on the corruption of the English language. 'Washeteria' by analogy with 'cafeteria' is possibly another.

Many of these coinages enjoy a vogue for a short period, but are not permanently adopted into the language. A number of recent additions to current speech and writing which have at least established themselves in *Chambers's Dictionary* are 'admass', the mass audience which advertisers seek to reach in commercial radio and TV; 'motel', a hotel made up of units each accommodating a car and its occupants; 'moped', a motor-assisted pedal cycle; and 'subtopia', a place where the city has sprawled into the country.

The American branch of English has always been a prolific source of vivid and often witty compounds which have been adopted on this side of the Atlantic. Fairly recent examples are 'tear-jerker', a song, film, or the like calling forth easy tears, and 'cliff-hanger', a thriller or ending line that leaves one in suspense. The vitality of our own slang, however, is attested in coinages such as 'never-never', a facetious term for hire-purchase, and 'skid-lid', a motor cyclist's crash helmet, a coinage which neatly utilizes the sound values of its components.

Compound coinages are more likely to appear more frequently in literary than in other kinds of prose, particularly in writers who like to experiment with language. We have already seen how Dylan Thomas compounded words in *Under Milk Wood*. Here is a passage from James Joyce's *Ulysses* which shows the same tendency:

> Their dog ambled about a bank of dwindling sand, trotting, sniffing on all sides. Looking for something lost in a past life. Suddenly he made off like a bounding hare, ears flung back, chasing the shadow of a lowskimming gull. The man's shrieked whistle struck his limp ears. He turned, bounded back, came nearer, trotted on twinkling shanks. On a field tenney a buck, trippant, proper unattired. At the lacefringe of the tide he halted with stiff forehoofs, seawardpointed ears. His snout lifted barked at the wavenoise, herds of seamorse.

The proportion of compounds in this short extract, 'lowskimming', 'lacefringe', 'seawardpointed', 'wavenoise', and 'seamorse', is far higher than we would find in most of the prose we encounter in daily life, and, indeed, in most literary English. It is noteworthy that at this point in the novel we see the scene from the point of view of Stephen Daedalus, and occasionally we even enter his consciousness, sharing his thoughts, as in the second sentence, and the sudden shift into the language of heraldry in the sixth. Stephen is portrayed as melancholy, sensitive, and poetic and hence the language is consistent with and appropriate to his character.

In literature Joyce probably carried experimentation with the word forms of language as far as it can possibly go. In *Ulysses* he described one day in the waking life of a number of characters in Dublin on 16 June 1904, and the material is presented in a brilliant but often bewildering variety of styles. Much of it makes use of a 'stream-of-consciousness' technique. In his last work, *Finnegan's Wake*, he tried to do for the night what he had done for the day in *Ulysses*, for the book is supposed to represent the dream-consciousness of a Dublin innkeeper as he lies asleep.

Just as in our dreams, images coalesce until we get composite figures made up of characteristics of two or more people, so in *Finnegan's Wake* words coalesce so that we get a telescoping of meaning, references to two or more things at the same time. Some examples taken at random are 'her furze-born sons', 'homogenius man', and at a more extended level, 'In the name of Annah the Allmazeful, the Everlasting, the Bringer of Plurabilities, haloed be her eve, her singtime sung, her rill be run, unhemmed as it is uneven'. (The innkeeper's wife, Anna, becomes in the dream world Anna Livia Plurabelle and is identified with the River Liffey upon which Dublin stands.) Notice how the language tries to catch the logic of the dream. Anna merges with Allah, the Allmerciful, and this religious association leads straight on to the rhythm of the Lord's Prayer, but to the sound of the river.

This can be quite amusing in small doses but the amount of effort required to elucidate all the references in any one sentence is so exhausting that *Finnegan's Wake* remains one of the great unread works of literature. However, Joyce's influence appears to have extended to the most unlikely people. Here, for instance, is the opening of a story called *Treasure Ivan*, a parody of R. L. Stevenson's famous masterpiece, published in 1964 in a small volume of sketches by John Lennon of the Beatles.

> In a little seashore pub in Bristow a ragged gathering of rags are drinking and making melly (before sailing to seas in serge of grate treashy on a sudden Isle far across the ocean).
> 'Belay there, me 'earty scabs,' says Large John Soliver entering. Pegging along towards some old saviours who have soled the several seas.

(You might care to consider which extract has most point.)

SYNTAX

Syntax is that part of the grammar of a language which concerns the order in which we arrange words in an utterance so that they make sense. In a highly inflected language (i.e. a language in which changes in the grammatical status of words are indicated by changes in the endings of the words themselves – Latin, for instance) the order in which words are introduced is not all that important. Chaucer's Prioress in the Prologue to the *Canterbury Tales*, you may remember, wore a brooch in which was written in Latin 'Amor Vincit Omnia' – Love Conquers All. It would still mean the same (although the emphasis would be slightly different) if it were written 'Omnia Vincit Amor', or 'Amor Omnia Vincit', since the inflections make it perfectly clear which word is the Subject and which the Object of the verb. On the other hand, in English, a language which at one time also had inflections but which has replaced nearly all of them by function words like 'of', 'by', 'with', 'from', 'to', etc., it may make all the difference in the world if we change the order of the words in a sentence. There is a very great divergence in meaning between 'Dog Bites Man' and 'Man Bites Dog'. Here the Subject of the sentence is determined by the order or the position of the word in the sequence.

THE BASIC STRUCTURE OF THE ENGLISH CLAUSE

The basic elements in an English clause are the Subject, Predicate, Complement(s), and Adjunct(s), and they normally appear in that order – SPCA. The Complement is an inclusive term incorporating the Object, the Indirect Object, and the Complement proper. An Adjunct is any kind of adverbial modifier. A simple sentence, one containing a single clause, indicates the usual pattern of these elements.

S	P	C	A
The caller	replaced	the telephone	on the hook

The normal pattern may be varied for a number of reasons. In poetry it is often done merely to suit the demands of the rhyme. In prose, however, it is more likely to be done to achieve particular effects. The important positions in a sentence, or a clause, tend to be the beginning and, to a lesser extent, the end. Hence, frequently the Complement is moved to the beginning of the sentence in order to emphasize that element. In the Gibbon passage we have already noted this in the clause, 'War he detested', CSP. This may also occur when the Complement is a clause. In 'How the rest of the congregation spent this fast I do not know', the entire first clause is the Complement of the verb 'know' and the same is the case in 'What little he had ever known, he had now forgotten completely'. (Try placing the two clauses in the normal order and notice how much of the effectiveness of the sentence is lost.) This shift of a clause Complement to the

beginning of a sentence is a very common feature of colloquial speech –
'How he ever got a game for England, I shall never know!'

The motive behind the inversion of the Subject and Complement
may simply be to provide a logical connection between two sentences.

Some members of the party wanted to nationalize the basic indus-
tries. Such people he called crypto-communists.

Here 'such people' has been moved to the beginning of the second
sentence to provide a close link with the first. The same technique may
be used to tie paragraphs together logically.

. . . As I left he asked me if I knew what had become of Standish.
What did become of Standish I have never discovered.

The transference of the clause to the initial position in the sentence
makes the transition from paragraph to paragraph smoother and underlines the connection between them.

Except for one position, the displacement of the Adjunct from its
normal place in the clause has less significance, since it is the most
variable of all the elements in the clause structure. When the Adjunct
occurs at the opening of a sentence, however, it can have an important
effect. Sometimes its appearance here does not seem to make much
difference except to give it a little more emphasis. For example 'In the
morning he rang his solicitor' does not seem all that different from
'He rang his solicitor in the morning'. But frequently when a writer
uses the Adjunct as an opening of his sentence it has a *thematic* function,
controlling the reader's attitude to the subsequent ideas; and frequently,
too, it has a *structural* function, marking a shift in the train of thought,
a new development of the argument.

So, if a writer chooses to begin a sentence with a number of similar
Adjuncts and further to invert the Subject and Predicator he is
obviously aiming at some subtle stylistic effect, as in this sentence
from Patrick White's *Riders in the Chariot*:

Out of its bower of rather unhappy exotic trees, out of its necklaces
of rosebuds . . . aspired the lovely languid house.

The inversion of Subject and Predicator with the Adjunct coming
first in the sentence is a relatively frequent variation with intransitive
verbs.

From the surface of the lake rose, wheeling, a flight of swans.

From her mouth ran a thin trickle of blood.

As we have said, the Adjunct is the most mobile of all the elements of the clause. This is particularly true if it consists of a single adverb. Consider, for example, the different positions it can occupy in the following sentences:

He had apparently lost his way.
He had lost his way, apparently.
Apparently, he had lost his way.
He, apparently, had lost his way.
He had lost, apparently, his way.

You might consider whether there are any differences in meaning caused by the movement of the adverb, or whether it is purely a question of altering the rhythm of the sentence. What do you consider the effect of the variations of normal word order to be in the following?

What some people call 'loaded' I am.

ZSA ZSA GABOR

If ever I forget your name, let me forget home and Heaven.

HARDY, The Woodlanders

We can see, too, how such alterations of the normal order can control or establish the reader's attitude to the remainder of the sentence or sentences that follow. For example, Walter Greenwood in *Love on the Dole* has

Hands in pockets, shoulders hunched, he would slink around the by streets to the billiard hall, glad to be somewhere out of the public gaze . . .

The inversions we have noticed in the Edmund Burke passage are characteristic of exclamatory sentences – 'Little did I dream . . .' and 'never, never more shall we behold . . .' – where the Subject is placed between the auxiliary and the main verb. Inversions such as these are more typical of literary or oratorical prose than of more informal styles of writing, where the forms would probably be 'I never dreamed . . .' and 'I never saw . . .' This is also true of the inversion after a negative as in this example, again from *The Decline and Fall of the Roman Empire*:

Since the foundation of Rome no general had more nobly deserved a triumph than Aurelian; nor was a triumph ever celebrated with superior pride and magnificence.

43

OMISSION OF ELEMENTS OF STRUCTURE

As well as being at liberty to vary the position of structural elements for stylistic or logical reasons, the writer may occasionally omit one element altogether, particularly the Predicator when it is part of the verb 'to be'. The effect of the omission is to make for greater compactness, or to relate separate ideas more closely, or to throw certain words into greater relief to impart additional force. In *Elizabeth and Essex*, for instance, Lytton Strachey, after quoting Essex's reply to charges brought against him by Queen Elizabeth, comments: 'Magnificent words certainly, but dangerous, portentous, and not wise'. The omission of 'These are' or 'These were' helps to increase the impact of the sentence since they add nothing in fact to the meaning which is not already implicit. (English, like most European languages, normally demands the inclusion of the verb 'to be' expressing some simple existing link between Subject and Complement whereas in the present tense Russian manages to get along without. A Russian simply says 'Here house', 'There door'.)

Similarly Aldous Huxley in one of his essays ends a paragraph with the sentence: 'Bernini is, spiritually speaking, a *plein-airiste*', and begins the next with 'Not so El Greco'. The concision achieved by the omission of the Predicator adds to the force of the contrast.

THE COMPLEX SENTENCE

As we have already seen, the typical English clause tends to have its heavily modified elements in the Complement rather than in the Subject. The complex sentence shows a similar tendency to concentrate the modifying clauses after rather than before the main clause, as this sentence from Scott's *Old Mortality* shows:

> The leading files of the regiment had nearly attained the brow of the steep hill we have mentioned, when two or three horsemen, speedily discovered to be a part of their own advanced guard, who had acted as a patrol, appeared returning at full gallop, their horses much blown, and the men apparently in a disordered flight.

The main clause introduces the sentence and the qualifying elements bring up the rear. This is a particularly illuminating sentence grammatically. Obviously the more important item of information conveyed by it is the appearance of the small party of horsemen. This information is transmitted, however, in a clause which technically is dependent or subordinate. The independent clause is the first, 'The leading files of the regiment had nearly attained the brow of the steep hill', but the information it contains is fairly obviously of less importance than what follows. This indicates that technical terms like 'principal' or 'main' clause are misleading if they suggest that there is a correlation between their technical names and the kind of information they convey. Scott could easily have restructured the sentence, making the first clause subordinate, e.g., 'When the leading files of the regiment had nearly attained the brow of the steep hill, two or three horsemen, speedily discovered to be a patrol . . .' and this might appear to be a more logical arrangement. But a subtle, almost imperceptible, shift has taken place in the meaning. In Scott's original version the two principal items of information have very nearly equal weight, so to speak, but in the amended version the first item seems to have become very much a subordinate fact.

Modern writers generally prefer a somewhat less complicated sentence structure than Scott but here is Iris Murdoch using the same basic pattern in *The Italian Girl*:

The bamboos had invaded the stream now, their straight strong stems grouped in the water itself, while the stream, more choked than ever with its debris of round grey stones, meandered a blackish brown under the sun-tinged arches.

This type of sentence is called a *loose* sentence. Contrasted with it is the *periodic* sentence where the main clause is delayed until the end and the meaning is suspended until the entire sentence is complete; as in this example from Hazlitt's essay *On Living to One's-self*:

If love at first sight were mutual, or to be conciliated by kind offices; if the fondest affection were not so often repaid and chilled by indifference and scorn; if so many lovers both before and since the madman in *Don Quixote* had not 'worshipped a statue, hunted the wind, cried aloud to the desert'; if friendship were lasting; if merit were renown and renown were health, riches, and long life; or if the homage of the world were to conscious worth and the true aspirations after excellence, instead of its gaudy signs and outward trappings; then indeed I might be of the opinion that it is better to live to others than one's-self.

Here a whole series of conditional clauses is piled up in front of the main clause, which completes the sense. (The punctuation of the sentence is also worth looking at.)

Just as the Adjunct frequently appears before the Subject in the clause, so a very common pattern of the complex sentence in English is one where an adverbial clause (or clauses) comes before the independent clause which is in turn followed by further subordinate clauses. This pattern is neither loose nor periodic but shares some of the characteristics of both. This example is from Dickens's *The Old Curiosity Shop*.

> While he, subdued and abashed, seemed to crouch before her, and to shrink and cower down as if in the presence of some superior creature, the child herself was sensible of a new feeling within her, which elevated her nature, and inspired her with an energy and confidence she had never known.

These three basic types of complex sentence do not, of course, appear in English in equal proportions. While loose and mixed sentences are very common, the periodic sentence appears only very rarely. To select examples of the first two one has only to open any book at random: to find a specimen of the periodic sentence one has to search for some time.

Loose and mixed sentences give the impression of an author improvising his thoughts as he goes along, while the writer of the periodic sentence must obviously know where he is going before he starts. Generally speaking, the writer who makes use of a fair proportion of periodic sentences is one who takes considerable care over his style while the writer who habitually uses only loose and mixed sentences suggests more spontaneity and liveliness.

As far as the relationship between writer and reader is concerned, loose and mixed sentences generally bring the two closer together while the periodic sentence seems to increase the distance between them. The former gives the reader the impression of being spoken *to*, the latter tends to give the impression of being spoken *at*.

BALANCED SENTENCES AND PARALLEL STRUCTURES

A rhetorical device which has been used in English since at least the sixteenth century is *antithesis* or the balanced sentence, where the second half of the sentence is a mirror of the first as far as grammatical structure is concerned while the ideas in the two halves are contrasted. Bacon began his essay *Of Travel* with the sentence:

> Travel in the younger sort, is a part of education: in the elder, a part of experience.

The balanced structure helps to point up the differences in the ideas expressed. It lends itself, of course, to the expression of wit in prose, as in Oscar Wilde's *The Decay of Lying*:

The ancient historians gave us delightful fiction in the form of fact: the modern novelist presents us with dull facts in the guise of fiction,

or Lady Bracknell's comment on being informed in *The Importance of Being Earnest* that Ernest Worthing is an orphan:

To lose one parent, Mr Worthing, may be regarded as a misfortune: to lose both looks like carelessness.

Wilde could also use triple parallel structures to good effect as when he wrote of the novelist George Meredith:

As a writer he has mastered everything except language: as a novelist he can do everything, except tell a story: as an artist he is everything except articulate.

The most sustained use of parallel structures, however, is probably found in Bacon's famous essay *Of Studies* which begins with a triple distinction and preserves this three-part structure throughout:

Studies serve for delight, for ornament, and for ability. Their chief use for delight is in privateness and retiring; for ornament, is in discourse; and for ability, is in the judgement and disposition of business. . . . To spend too much time in Studies is sloth; to use them too much for ornament, is affectation; to make judgement wholly by their rules, is the humour of a scholar . . . crafty men condemn studies; simple men admire them; and wise men use them. . . . Some books are to be tasted, others to be swallowed, and some few to be chewed and digested. . . . Reading maketh a full man; conference a ready man; and writing an exact man. . . .

Writing as schematic as this is obviously more suited to expository than to imaginative writing. One of its advantages is that it acts, like rhyme and rhythm in poetry, to make the sentences memorable, as we can see in this extract from Gibbon's *Autobiography*:

Freedom is the first wish of our heart; freedom is the first blessing of our nature; and unless we blind ourselves with the voluntary chains of interest or passion, we advance in freedom as we advance in years.

When it occurs in personal writing, however, it may have a cold, distancing effect. Elsewhere in his *Autobiography* Gibbon described how his father refused him permission to marry a lady he had met in Switzerland:

> At Crassy and Lausanne I indulged my dream of felicity: but on my return to England, I soon discovered that my father would not hear of this strange alliance, and that without his consent, I was myself destitute and helpless. After a painful struggle I yielded to my fate; I sighed as a lover, I obeyed as a son; my wound was insensibly healed by time, absence, and the habits of a new life.

This passage is elegant and dignified, but the studied cadences of the passage, and particularly the antithesis, 'I sighed as a lover; I obeyed as a son', do not suggest any overpowering ardour in the young Gibbon.

THE SIGNIFICANCE OF SENTENCE STRUCTURE

It is very difficult to define just *precisely* what contribution the sentence structure of a passage makes to its general significance, and very little work has been done upon this aspect of style. What conclusions can be drawn from the length and complexity of the sentence structure? (Length and complexity are not necessarily the same thing; a long sentence may well have a very simple structure.)

What conclusions we come to will depend a great deal, of course, on *what kind* of writing it is, and what kind of effect the writer is trying to achieve. When a writer is presenting action, for example, it is generally true to say that the use of short sentences will tend to reinforce the sense of the speed of events. This passage, for instance, from Hemingway's *A Farewell to Arms*, describes how Lieutenant Henry, an American serving with the Italian Medical Corps, escapes when in imminent danger of being shot as a deserter:

> I looked at the carabinieri. They were looking at the newcomers. The others were looking at the colonel. I ducked down, pushed between two men, and ran for the river, my head down. I tripped at the edge and went in with a splash. The water was very cold and I stayed under as long as I could. I could feel the current swirl me and I stayed under until I thought I could never come up. The minute I came up I took a breath and went down again. It was easy to stay under with so much clothing and my boots. When I came up the second time I saw a piece of timber ahead of me and reached

it and held on with one hand. I kept my head behind it and did not even look over it. I did not want to see the bank.

Hemingway's short, crisp sentences certainly suggest the explosive speed of the escape. On the other hand, this extract from William Faulkner's *Intruder in the Dust* also suggests the rush of action but this time it is conveyed by one long breathless sentence:

> He would remember it: watching the old man clap the pistol again butt-forward into his armpit and clamp it there with the stump of the arm while the one hand unbuttoned the shirt then took the pistol from the armpit and thrust it back inside the shirt then buttoned the shirt again then turned even faster quicker than the two sons half his age, already in front of everybody when he hopped back over the fence and went to the mare and caught reins and pommell all in one hand, already swinging up: then the two cars dropping in second speed against gravity back down the steep pitch until he said 'Here' where the pickup's tracks slewed off the road into the bushes then back into the road again and his uncle stopped: and he watched the fierce old stump-armed man jump the buckskin mare up out of the road into the woods on the opposite side already falling away down towards the branch, then the two hounds flowing up the bank behind him and then the mule with the two identical wooden-faced sons on it: then he and his uncle were out of the car the sheriff's car bumper to bumper behind them, hearing the mare crashing on down towards the branch and then the old man's high flat voice shouting at the hounds:
> 'Hi! Hi! Hum on boy! At him, Ring!' and then his uncle: 'Handcuff them through the steering wheel': and then the sheriff: 'No. We'll need the shovels': and he had climbed the bank too, listening off and downwards towards the crashing and shouts, then his uncle and the sheriff and the two negroes carrying the shovels were beside him.

The entire action from the moment the one-armed old man places the pistol under his armpit until the small group forms at the top of the bank is conveyed as one continuous panoramic spectacle, the individual items of the panorama being short simple sentence units linked by repeated simple connectives, particularly 'then'. Yet it is the feeling of headlong action that is conveyed, not by the length of the sentence but by the structure that is employed within it.

Therefore while we should always be alert to note that as a general rule when a writer employs short simple separate sentences in series he may be aiming at speed of narration of action, a similar speed effect may well be obtained by structuring simple sentence units in other ways, as in Faulkner's very long sentence. It must be observed, of course, that Faulkner is employing a special technique. Normally the longer types of sentence have a fairly complex structure that slows the reader's mind by a closer interrelation of the ideas, punctuated to force pauses, all this giving the impression that things happen in a more leisurely way.

Incidentally, it is as well to notice another aspect in which the two passages differ – the point of view of the narrator. In the Hemingway passage the narrator relates the events in the first person as a direct participant in the action, thus conferring the immediacy we associate with the eye-witness account in which personal impression succeeds personal impression. The succession of simple short sentences fits the point of view. Faulkner has set himself a different and perhaps more difficult task. His narrator stands outside the action and narrates as the third person onlooker. But he wants to present the sequence of events so that the reader will feel he is seeing it through the eyes of the young boy. Hence the simple sentence units, joined by simple connectives, and particularly by the use of 'then' – typical of the young immature storyteller – are admirable devices for displaying the scenes as filtered through the boy's consciousness. Thus though the effect is less immediate than in the Hemingway we, the readers, still see it with a rapidity of happening and as the boy experienced it.

Hemingway, as a principle of writing, deliberately stripped his language to the bone, intending to gain impact from presenting to the reader the essential skeleton of the human experience. The power so generated could be reinforced by the structural device of the short sentence. Thus he could take the individual skeleton units of the human experience and by short sentence units arrange them in the precise patterns that would suit his story-telling purpose.

Thus it is not possible to rank writers on a sort of league table of merit based on the complexity of their sentence structure, for Hemingway, at his best a very fine writer, would certainly be at the bottom of the league.

The complexity of the sentence structure may, on the other hand, mirror the complexity and subtlety of the writer's thought. This is particularly true in discursive or expository prose where the writer is handling ideas and may wish to introduce qualifications and provisos. It can, however, be found in imaginative literature as well. Compare the elaboration of this passage from Henry James's *The Golden Bowl* with the simplicity of Hemingway. Charlotte Verver, second wife of a very rich American, watches the entry of her husband's son-in-law, Prince Amerigo, an Italian prince, into a party given by her husband.

When presently, therefore, from her standpoint, she saw the Prince come back she had an impression of all the place as higher and wider and more appointed for great moments; with its dome of lustres lifted, its ascents and descents more majestic, its marble tiers more vividly overhung, its numerosity of royalties, foreign and domestic, more unprecedented, its symbolism of 'State' hospitality both emphasized and refined. This was doubtless a large consequence of a fairly familiar cause, a considerable stir to spring from the mere vision, striking as that might be, of Amerigo in a crowd; but she had her reasons, she held them there, she carried them in fact, responsibly and overtly, as she carried her head, her high tiara, her folded fan, her indifferent, unattended eminence; and it was when he reached her and she could, taking his arm, show herself as placed in her relation, that she felt supremely justified. It was her notion, of course, that she gave a glimpse of but few of her grounds for this discrimination – indeed of the most evident alone: yet she would have been half-willing it should be guessed how she drew inspiration, drew support, in quantity sufficient for almost anything, from the individual value that, through all the picture, her husband's son-in-law kept for the eye, deriving it from his fine unconscious way, in the swarming social sum of outshining, overlooking and overtopping.

The contrast between the elemental thoughts of Lt. Henry and the subtle, sophisticated mental processes of Charlotte Verver could hardly be more marked. Hemingway was drawn to depict strong, silent often inarticulate heroes; Henry James delighted in the exploration of the most refined and discriminating consciousnesses. It could be argued in fact that Henry James in the passage has almost refined consciousness out of existence! For the average intelligent reader it requires several careful perusals to determine just exactly what the author is saying, and yet on examination we find that the whole thing is admirably controlled, every detail and every qualification fitting neatly into the complicated structure of each sentence. A rough précis of the paragraph would be that for Charlotte the hall in which the ceremony was taking place seemed to grow larger and more majestic with the arrival of the prince; a large claim to make from the simple fact of his appearance in a crowd, and yet justified for her because of his evident superiority over everybody else. But how much more there is in the paragraph as we watch it through Charlotte's consciousness! (Incidentally, both Hemingway and Henry James were Americans, although the latter in his later years became a naturalized British citizen, like T. S. Eliot after him. The American critic Philip Rahv has divided American writers into two categories, Redskins and Palefaces. Is there any doubt about the placing of these two?)

THE USE OF CONNECTIVES IN PROSE

As we have seen, Hemingway rarely uses any connectives except 'and', 'the most non-committal of conjunctions', as it has been described. When a writer of Hemingway's calibre chooses to restrict himself in this way, it does seem as if he were implying that things happen one after another without any necessary connection between them. Events occur in a temporal sequence and that is all. If a writer on the other hand uses conjunctions like 'thus', 'therefore', 'so that', and so on, it does suggest that events are somehow inter-connected, that there is a pattern of cause and effect in the world.

Particularly in expository prose – prose which is intended to explain something to the reader – it is useful to examine carefully the writer's use of conjunctions and other connectives as a clue to the structure of his argument. Once again the perceptive Coleridge highlights the important function these perform:

> A close reasoner and a good writer in general may be known by his pertinent use of connectives. Read a page of Johnson; you cannot alter one conjunction without spoiling the sense. In your modern books for the most part, the sentences in a page have the same connection with each other that marbles have in a bag; they touch without adhering.

How then does the writer ensure that his sentences not only touch but adhere, that each one follows logically from the next?

There are three principal means of providing a piece of explanatory or argumentative prose with a logical and coherent structure. First, there is the use of conjunctions, adverbs, and adverbial phrases which indicate relationships between statements. The relationships they indicate will be of different kinds. They may simply refer to the addition of further facts or instances: 'and', 'too', 'also', 'likewise', 'in addition', 'moreover'. They may indicate an opposing relation: 'but', 'on the contrary', 'on the other hand'. Or again they may indicate some purposeful or causal relation: 'so', 'so that', 'as a result', 'therefore', 'consequently', 'thus'. These are only a few of the logical relationships between statements which can be conveyed by simple connectives. Thus in any piece of prose, and particularly in discursive, or argumentative or persuasive prose, it is important that we should observe the writer's use of connectives and how far they are used to condition the responses, including intellectual responses, of the reader.

Secondly, the writer may guide the reader from sentence to sentence and paragraph to paragraph by repeating words and phrases verbatim, for example:

All of these factors result in a condition of *social unrest and economic uncertainty* which seem to presage the end of our civilization.

Social unrest and economic uncertainty, however, are not always an unhealthy condition.

The first sentence of a paragraph is linked to the final sentence of the previous paragraph by the simple repetition of a phrase, while the adverb 'however' indicates the logical relationship. Sometimes the idea is repeated but rephrased to avoid the direct repetition of the example above.

Such words are called 'learned' and the *distinction* between them and the 'popular' words is of great importance to a right understanding of linguistic process.

The *difference* between popular and learned words may be easily seen in a few examples.

Thirdly, the same effect of tying sentences and paragraphs together into a coherent whole may be achieved by the use of pronouns, particularly the demonstratives 'this', 'that', 'these', and 'those', 'the former', 'the latter' and words like 'such' and 'similar'. 'Social unrest and economic uncertainty' in the first example quoted could well be repeated as '*Such a situation*, however, is not always an unhealthy condition'.

The following passage from a textbook of elementary psychology illustrates all of these devices as the writer welds his paragraph into a coherent whole:

As mentioned previously, intelligence may be defined as the *ability* to profit from previous experience. But there is no guarantee that *such ability* will be used. *Thus* in the case of a criminal, we may deduce from the masterly way in which his activities are conceived and executed that he has a high level of intelligence, planning and executive ability; *yet* in spite of his ability, he may be *repeatedly arrested, gaoled, hunted, and have a very unpleasant time* indeed. The case for turning his talents to better use may be convincingly put to him, and he may agree that in his particular case crime has not paid. He may, *however*, and all too frequently does, fail to profit from his *unfortunate experiences*, and again return to a life of crime. The reason for *this* is sought by *some* in a psychoanalytical explanation. The blame may be placed on an unsympathetic stepmother. *Others* may hold society responsible for the production of criminals, seeing in the current vogue of violence in American films, literature, drama, and radio the source of the juvenile delinquency which so rapidly produces the hardened criminal. Be *that* as it may, it is clear that intelligence is but one of the qualities which enable people to make a success of their lives, to live reasonably happily and to be useful citizens – three things which are not always the same thing.

The structure of this paragraph follows a logical pattern. The theme is the assertion that, while intelligence may be the ability to profit from previous experience, this ability will not necessarily be used, and this appears in the first sentence, with its definition of intelligence, and the second with its counter-statement. The writer then proceeds to give a concrete instance to illustrate the point; the intelligent criminal who repeatedly returns to illegal activities. Two possible explanations of this behaviour are then introduced, the psychoanalytical and the environmental, and the paragraph is rounded off with the conclusion that can be drawn from the evidence adduced, that intelligence is only one of the factors contributing to success in life.

Within the paragraph the reader is guided through the development of the ideas by the devices we described earlier. To make it easier to follow, the relevant words have been italicized. The relationship between the two initial sentences is, of course, indicated by the conjunction 'but' and the two are linked by the repetition of 'ability' plus 'such' in the second. 'Thus' introduces the illustrative example, within which the contrast between the criminal's obvious intelligence and his conduct is pinpointed by the use of 'yet' and 'however'. 'He may be repeatedly arrested, gaoled, hunted' in the third sentence is condensed and rephrased as 'his unfortunate experiences' in the fifth. When the writer proceeds to examine possible causes, the pronoun 'this' refers back to his odd behaviour. Two different possible explanations are provided linked by 'some' and 'others'. Finally, 'Be that as it may', ('that' being the ultimate responsibility), links the conclusion to the rest of the paragraph.

We have now spent enough time on the grammatical structures of English and their significance. On the subtler effects of syntax, almost inexplicable in analytical terms, perhaps Bertolt Brecht, the German playwright, should have the last word. Brecht claimed that he had worked out a special technique for the speaking of prose or verse which he called *gestisch* in German. By this he meant a language in which the words already contain the gestures that must accompany them. He illustrated what he meant by a quotation from the Bible: to say 'Pluck out the eye that offends thee' is far less effective than 'If thine eye offend thee, pluck it out'.

Exercises on Grammar

Examine the sentence structure and other grammatical elements of the following and try to assess what they contribute to the meaning (you may, of course, comment on any other features which seem to you to be significant):

1. The great Whig country houses of the eighteenth and early nineteenth centuries are among the most conspicuous monuments of English history. Ornate and massive, with their pedimented porticoes, their spreading balustraded wings, they dominate the landscape round them with a magnificent self-assurance. Nor are their interiors less imposing. Their colonnaded entrance halls, whence the Adam staircase sweeps up beneath a fluted dome; their cream and gilt libraries piled with sumptuous editions of the classics; their orangeries peopled with casts from the antique; their salons hung with yellow silk, and with ceiling and doorways painted in delicate arabesque by Angelica Kauffmann, all combine to produce an extraordinary impression of culture and elegance and established power.

   DAVID CECIL, *The Young Melbourne*

2. Twilight over meadow and water, the eve-star shining above the hill, and Old Nog the heron crying kra-aark! as his slow dark wings carried him down to the estuary. A whiteness drifting above the sere reeds of the riverside, for the owl had flown from under the middle arch of the stone bridge that once had carried the canal across the river.

   HENRY WILLIAMSON, *Tarka the Otter*

3. In the character of his Elegy I rejoice to concur with the common reader; for by the common sense of readers uncorrupted with literary prejudices, after all the refinements of subtility and the dogmatism of learning, must be finally decided all claim to poetical honours. The churchyard abounds with images which find a mirror in every mind, and with sentiments to which every bosom returns an echo. The four stanzas beginning 'Yet even these bones' are to me original: I have never seen the notions in any other place; yet he that reads them here, persuades himself that he has always felt them. Had Gray written often thus, it had been vain to blame, and useless to praise him.

SAMUEL JOHNSON, Lives of the English Poets

4. Wide-fronted distant prospect of Welsh hill over there beyond the Severn valley. Haresfield Beacon in the middle-distance, with tufts of trees on top, like a clown's hair. Woldstone Village, a twentieth-century road through a nineteenth-century maze. The broad rustic burr of Gloucestershire voices. Villagers equable and kindly, yet always a little aloof, as if our green caps and grey uniforms made us different creatures, kept in special circumstances. Straw hats and Sunday walks. Round the brickworks chimney. Up Doverow. Three miles exactly. 'Which would you rather do – run a mile, jump a stile, or eat a pancake in a field?' 'Eat a pancake in a field.' 'Eat this then!' – and the flat round cake of cow-dung is throw at his head. Laughter. 'Keep in the crocodile, Bevan!' 'Yes, sir. Sorry, sir.' Tuckshop. Mars Bars. 'Keep in line there – Mrs Brown can't serve you all at once!' 'Yes, sir. Sorry, sir.' But I had advanced three places. 'Please, sir – can I go to the bog?' 'You may go to the lavatory if you must, but I have told you before not to employ that disgusting schoolboy slang.'

PETER FORSTER, Play the Ball

5. Only the steady creaking of a flight of swans disturbed the silence, labouring low overhead with outstretched necks towards the sea. It was a warm, wet, windless afternoon with a soft, feathery feeling in the air: rain, yet so fine it could scarcely fall but floated. It clung to everything it touched; the rushes in the deep choked ditches of the sea-marsh were bowed down with it, the small black cattle looked cobwebbed with it, their horns were jewelled with it. Curiously

stumpy too these cattle looked, the whole herd sunk nearly to the knees in a soft patch.

RICHARD HUGHES, *The Fox in the Attic*

6. . . . and we played the battle of Port Arthur in the bathtub and the water leaked down through the drawingroom ceiling and it was altogether too bad but in Kew Gardens old Mr Garnet who was still hale and hearty although so very old came to tea and we saw him first through the window with his red face and John Bull whiskers and Aunty said it was a sailor's rolling gait and he was carrying a box under his arm and Vickie and Pompon barked and here was Mr Garnet come to tea and he took a gramophone out of a black box and put a cylinder on the gramophone and they pushed back the teathings off the corner of the table. Be careful not to drop it now they scratch rather heasy. Why a hordinary sewin' neddle would do maam but I 'ave special needles.

JOHN DOS PASSOS, *The 42nd Parallel*

The Element of Meaning

In examining the significance of the language of prose we have been considering so far the elements of sound and grammar, the two which are most likely to be overlooked, since their operation is much more subtle and unobtrusive than that of the last element we have now to consider, the element of meaning. This is by far the most important of the three since it is principally through the exploration of the 'meaning' of words that a writer conveys his message to his readers.

THE MEANING OF MEANING

First, however, we might do well to look at the meaning of 'meaning' itself. On the face of it, this seems an absurdly simple problem but, when we start trying to define meaning rigorously, we find ourselves in all sorts of philosophical tangles. Fortunately there is no need for us to go into the question in such depth here. However, in asking ourselves what is signified by the 'meaning' of a word, there are problems even if we confine ourselves to 'common-sense' answers such as 'the meaning of a word is what it refers to' or 'the meaning of word is the definition provided by the dictionary'.

In the first place, some words seem to have more meaning than others. While most of us would have little difficulty in hazarding some sort of suggestion as to what words like 'table', 'chair', 'courage', 'enter', 'slender', refer to, how many of us would feel competent to express the meaning of 'if', 'so', 'whether', 'but'? The latter group, selected from the relatively small number of function words which provide the basic structure of our language, seem to have logical meaning rather than an intrinsic meaning of their own. They express the relationships between the nouns, verbs, adjectives, and adverbs of the first group.

In the second place, most words do not have *a* meaning but several, and some have a very large number of them. In fact the more frequently a word is used in speech and writing the more meanings it is likely to acquire. One linguist, indeed, claims to have discovered a statistical relation between the frequency of a word and the number of meanings attributed to it, the latter being proportional to the square root of the frequency. However sceptical we may be of the possibility of quantifying meaning with such mathematical precision, we must concede that there is a general correlation between frequency of occurrence and multiplicity of meaning. The *Oxford English Dictionary* lists 69 different senses of the verb 'to come', 94 for 'go', and 97 for 'make'. The Thorndike Word List records words, not alphabetically, but in order of the frequency of their occurrence. The total number of different meanings given, with examples of use, in the *O.E.D.* for the first 500 words in the Thorndike List is 14,070, an average of 28 for each. Even if the first 1,000 words are taken, the average has only decreased slightly to 25.

Very often the different meanings of a word are closely related to one another, have a sort of family likeness, or are obvious extensions of an original meaning. It is fairly clear, for instance, how the word 'board', beginning as a broad, thin sheet of timber, becomes a table, and then the food that is placed upon the table as in 'bed and board'. Again the table may be a large one round which a council of some sort may sit and the meaning may be extended to the people who sit round it as in 'the Electricity Board'. Sometimes the relationship is far from clear as in the different meanings of 'pupil' – 'one who is taught', and 'the centre of the eye'. In fact the first meaning is derived from the small image seen in the pupil of the eye. Sometimes the meanings *are* totally unrelated as in 'punch' – 'a blow with the fist', and 'a kind of mixed drink'. In this case we are really dealing with two different words from separate derivations which happen to be spelt and to sound alike.

THE IMPORTANCE OF CONTEXT

In normal circumstances we have no difficulty in deciding which of the possible meanings of a word is the relevant one, since this is determined by either the *verbal context* or the *context of situation*, that is, by the other words surrounding the word in question, or the situation in which we hear it uttered. The precise shade of meaning that the writer has in mind or the use of a word in a specialized sense rather than a general one will be obvious from either or both of these factors. For example, if we find the words 'company', 'interest', 'share', 'security', and 'stock' together in a verbal context, their specialized commercial meanings are likely to rise in our consciousness rather than the other unspecialized meanings which they all have. Similarly the context of situation would determine whether a man 'backing a horse' was a stableboy pursuing his normal duties or a punter having a flutter.

The fact that words have a multiplicity of meanings has caused some people to complain of the slipperiness of language, to infer that it is not to be trusted. The truth is, of course, that it is precisely this multiplication of meanings which makes language the powerful and flexible tool that it is. If for every conceptual nuance a separate term had to be provided, language would become unwieldy and the process of communication extremely difficult, like learning to write Chinese, a language in which you have to learn the character for every word separately, since it has no alphabet. Of course, because a word may have a multiplicity of meanings, there is always the danger of ambiguity, but it is the writer's job so to manipulate the verbal context that the unwanted connotations do not arise in the reader's mind.

The writer may *wish* to make use of ambiguity for various purposes, serious or comic. The pun is a figure of speech based on the fact that words have more than one meaning, and, although condemned as the lowest form of wit, it had a fascination for literary artists from Shakespeare to Oscar Wilde. Ingenious double and even triple puns can be perpetrated, particularly when words which sound the same are used, as in the case of the Texas millionaire who bought his sons a cattle-ranch which he called 'Focus' because, as he said, 'It's where the sons raise meat'.

The *double entendre* is another linguistic device which depends on the multiple meaning of words. Many a West End farce, or radio or TV comedy series, would be in dire straits if it were forced to dispense with this method of raising a laugh. The *double entendre* usually operates by having a second meaning which is vaguely rude or indecent and involves the maintenance of an air of complete innocence by the perpetrator.

Even in everyday life the potential ambiguity of language can be a help in trying situations. A well-known and respected Edinburgh professor suffered from having unsolicited and unwanted manuscripts and books sent to him. In self-defence he devised a verbal formula in replying to the donors which covered all eventualities. 'Thank you very much for the book. I shall certainly waste no time in reading it.' Similarly, faced with the problem of proving a reference for a member of staff whose diligence was rather suspect, an employer wrote: 'anyone who gets Mr A—— to work for him will be very lucky indeed'.

IRONY

It is even possible to manipulate language so that you say one thing and yet make it clear that you mean the opposite. This rhetorical device is known as *irony*. The essential thing about irony is that it operates at two levels and there is a contradiction between the two levels. This differentiates it from allegory which also operates at more than one level, one literal, the other or others implied, but there is no contradiction. Thus Christian's journey in *The Pilgrim's Progress* is on the literal level a real physical journey and implicitly a figurative account of the spiritual trials and tribulations of the Christian soul. George Orwell's *Animal Farm* is literally about the farm animals' revolt against the farmer, but allegorically about the Russian revolution. Allegory is at one with irony in this respect, however, that it is the implied or secondary meaning that is the important one. The literal meaning is the vehicle for conveying the significant comment.

A fairly crude form of irony is common in everyday speech. If we say, 'You're a bright character!' and indicate by the tone of voice we use that we mean exactly the opposite, we are using *sarcasm*, which is an elementary form of irony intended to hurt the recipient in some way. In prose, of course, the writer does not have the aid of tones of voice to indicate that he is being ironical. Hence irony can be a very dangerous weapon; the writer's assertions may be taken at their face value unless he is careful to make it clear to the reader that two levels of meaning are intended. The correspondence columns of newspapers, particularly the 'quality' press, frequently contain cries of horror and indignation from readers who have failed to appreciate that a letter-writer has been indulging in irony.

Swift is the great master of irony in English prose, as this extract from *Gulliver's Travels* will show:

> In the School of Political Projectors I was but ill entertained, the Professors appearing in my Judgement wholly out of their Senses, which is a scene that never fails to make me melancholy. These unhappy People were proposing Schemes for persuading Monarchs to chuse Favourites upon the score of their Wisdom, Capacity, and Virtue; of teaching Ministers to consult the Publick Good; of rewarding Merit, great Abilities and eminent Services; of instructing Princes to know their true Interest by placing it on the same foundation with that of the People: Of chusing for Employments Persons qualified to exercise them; with many other wild impossible Chimaeras, that never entered before into the heart of Man to con-

ceive, and confirmed me in the old Observation, that there is nothing so extravagant and irrational which some Philosophers have not maintained for Truth.

Swift's rejection as visionary and unrealistic of what is manifestly eminently reasonable and desirable makes his satire all the more effective. Here there can be no misunderstanding the ironic tone of the author. The dangers of misunderstanding, however, are illustrated in this extract from an essay on Education by Aldous Huxley:

If the mind is a mere receptacle which can be filled mechanically, as one fills a jug with water, it follows that a child who does not learn remains ignorant only through lack of good will; he deliberately closes his mental box, he refuses, malignantly, to admit the knowledge which his teachers are trying to pump into it. There is only one remedy: he must be compelled to open his mind, the opposing will must be broken – by moral persuasion, by threats, by physical torture. The fine old system of mechanical repetitive teaching, tempered by flagellation, was developed and perfected through the centuries.

This passage appeared in a schools examination some years ago. A surprising number of candidates accepted the initial premise that the mind is a mere receptacle, and the conclusions that followed from it, and deduced that Huxley also approved of this method of education because of his use of the phrase 'The fine old system', whereas Huxley meant 'fine' to be read as meaning its opposite.

THE AFFECTIVE CONNOTATIONS OF WORDS

So far we have been looking only at the informative connotations of words, the things they refer to. Many words, however, are also endowed with strong emotive or affective connotations; they not only provide us with information, they affect us in different ways. Language is an instrument which we use not only for reasoning about and describing our world but for evaluating it. Through language we can not only communicate facts about reality but can express judgements about it. The emotive aspect of language may indeed predate the informative. The origins of human language are hidden in the mists of pre-history and we will never be able to prove conclusively how speech began, but it is reasonable to suppose that language may have developed out of things like the cries early man uttered to warn the tribe of impending danger. Animals warn one another by a sort of emotional contagion when danger is present. Man can specify *what* the danger is. In any case, whatever the origin of language, as far as literature is concerned, poetry, the predominantly emotive use of language, certainly predates prose, which is a sophisticated and relatively late achievement in man's mastery of the process of communication.

Some words in English are almost entirely emotive or evaluative. They provide no information about the things they are applied to but tell us a lot about the feelings of the user. Some such words are 'nice', 'lovely', 'pleasant', 'splendid', 'marvellous', 'horrid', 'dreadful'. Others combine informative and emotive connotations; they have an evaluative element as an integral part of the meaning. To 'scribble', for instance, is 'to write badly, carelessly, or worthlessly' and thus includes a judgement on the kind of writing. Similarly a 'screech' is 'a harsh, shrill cry'.

As we have seen the context determines which particular informative connotation of a word rises into the consciousness. The same appears to be true of the affective connotations of words. Certain words seem to be inherently emotive and yet their emotive charge in certain contexts is not released. The word 'home' in English (neither French nor German has an exact equivalent) carries a very high potential emotive charge in most contexts – 'Home, sweet home', 'For England, home and beauty' – but it remains dormant in 'The Home Office'. Compare also the use of 'provincial' in 'The London and Provincial Bank', or 'He was made provincial governor' with 'He could not bear the provincial atmosphere of the town'. Similar contexts could be devised for a word like 'suburban'.

The emotive overtones of words can, of course, be pleasant or unpleasant, and the intensity of the feeling tone can vary as well, ranging from faint to extreme approval or disapproval. Bertrand Russell once continued the conjugation of the sentence 'I am firm' as 'You are stubborn' and 'He is a pig-headed fool', showing how the judgements become less and less favourable as the distance from the speaker increases. Exactly the same facts can be presented very differently depending on the nature of the emotive overtones of the words selected. The same person may be described as slender, slim, scrawny, lissom, stringy, scraggy or skinny by different observers according to taste. It is often possible to arrange words on a scale of increasing or decreasing approval or disapproval such as 'buxom', 'plump', 'stout', 'overweight', 'Junoesque', 'fat', 'obese'.

How very different attitudes to the same facts can be induced by the careful selection and manipulation of language can be seen from the two following passages on the patronage of the arts:

It has often been alleged, by self-styled lovers of painting or music or literature, that we are a nation of Philistines, and that nothing gives clearer proof of this than our government's grudging subsidy of the arts. Of course, we are told, these things are much better ordered elsewhere; in Scandinavia, for example, where state-supported theatres boldly face the difficulties of staging unmarketable plays, and where young painters and musicians are awarded scholarships of remarkable amplitude enabling them to do in France or Italy what they would otherwise have done at home. Unhappy Britain! – whose musicians sing in vain for their subsidies, and whose painters pine for want of parliamentary provision.

People with a genuine concern for painting or music or literature have often suggested that our government might be more generous in its subsidy of the arts, if only to defend us against the charge of being a nation of Philistines. They rightly point out that better provisions for the arts are made in other countries; in Scandinavia, for example, where state-supported theatres are able to present the kind of drama that is seen all too seldom on the commercial stage, and where talented young painters and musicians are endowed with grants enabling them to study under the most distinguished teachers, whether at home or abroad. It says little indeed, for Great Britain that our most promising students of music and painting must complete their training and develop their talents in comparative privation.

In order to reveal exactly how the different effects have been attained it is advisable to do two things; first, to list the *facts* communicated by each passage, and second, to examine the devices used in each to induce the particular attitudes each writer wishes to convey.

Both passages agree that Britain is less generous than other countries in subsidizing the arts, and has therefore incurred the charge of being a nation of Philistines. Both cite Scandinavia as an example of a country in which state-supported theatres stage plays not presented by the commercial theatre and provide scholarships for painters and musicians enabling them to study under distinguished teachers at home or abroad.

The two writers have, however, expressed contrary attitudes to these facts common to both. The first writer approves of the British government's behaviour and is at pains to discredit those critical of it. The second writer disapproves of the niggardliness of the government and defends the critics. The first begins by using the verb 'alleged' which immediately casts doubt on the validity of the charge made since what is alleged has still to be proved. Then the lovers of the arts are characterized as 'self-styled' which suggests doubts about their credentials as authorities on the arts. This contrasts with the second writer for whom the critics are 'people with a genuine concern'. The comparison with other countries is introduced in the first with the words 'Of course, we are told', the tone of which suggests that the writer is rather sceptical of the value of the evidence presented, while the second awards its seal of approval with the words 'They rightly point out'. The tone of the first becomes increasingly ironic; the State-supported theatre 'boldly faces the difficulty of staging *unmarketable* plays' which implies that the plays are at least of doubtful quality for otherwise they would be presented on the commercial stage. The second implies that plays staged by the state theatres are superior to those in the repertory of the commercial theatre. The second describes the grants as allowing young artists to study under 'the most distinguished teachers at home and abroad' thus emphasizing their value, but the first with its qualification of the scholarships as being 'of remarkable amplitude' and the insinuation that travel abroad is unnecessary, implies that they are a waste of money. Finally the first writer rounds off his attack with the heavy irony of the exclamatory introduction to his last sentence reinforced by the comic alliteration. The second writer comes down firmly on the side of the critics with the phrase 'it says little for Britain'.

Thus we see how, by the selection and manipulation of language, the same facts can be presented but entirely different attitudes to them evoked.

THE RESOURCES AVAILABLE TO THE WRITER

The English language is particularly rich in synonyms, words having approximately the same meaning. The cause of this richness lies to a large extent in the history of the English people. In its early history Britain was subjected to invasions by Romans, Angles and Saxons (who brought the English language with them), Danes and Norman French, and during the Renaissance the language suffered a classical cultural invasion, assimilating a great number of words from Greek and Latin. Again English has always been ready to borrow from another language if it required to coin a word for a new concept. In contrast German, which belongs to the same family of language as English, prefers to create a new word from native roots. For example, English 'Television', a hybrid derived partly from Greek and partly from Latin, is in German *Fernsehen* which would correspond to our calling TV 'Farseeing'.

Some language cranks have suggested that words which come from the old Anglo-Saxon stock are somehow 'purer' than words derived from the classical languages, and they have proposed native derivatives for terms which exist only in classical form, for example, 'pushwainling' for 'perambulator'.

No English writer can help using a mixture of words of native Anglo-Saxon origin and of foreign origin, but the proportions of the two in any passage will tend to vary according to the writer or the kind of writing he is engaged in. In so far as it is possible to generalize, the native English terms, for obvious reasons, tend to be more familiar and homelier, while the classical derivatives have a learned, abstract air. Scholarly and scientific works will, therefore, generally contain a fairly high percentage of the latter. Since the classical terms also tend to be rather bigger words than the native terms, they are often easily recognizable whether we have any knowledge of Latin or Greek or not. A further distinction between the native term and the classical derivative is that the former, since it is normally concerned with the basic human needs and desires, tends to have a warmer feeling tone and hence occurs rather more frequently in poetry and works of creative imaginative prose.

A comparison of the two following passages, the first from the Bible and the second from Sir James Frazer's great anthropological work *The Golden Bough*, shows clearly the contrast between prose which is basically Anglo-Saxon and heavily Latinized prose:

Now when Jacob saw that there was corn in Egypt, Jacob said unto his sons, Why do ye look upon one another? And he said, Behold, I have heard that there is corn in Egypt: get you down thither and buy for us from thence; that we may live, and not die. And Joseph's ten brethren went down to buy corn in Egypt. But Benjamin, Joseph's brother, Jacob sent not with his brethren; for he said, Lest peradventure mischief befall him.

But as time goes on this explanation in its turn proves to be unsatisfactory. For it assumes that the succession of natural events is not determined by immutable laws, but is to some extent variable and irregular, and this assumption is not borne out by closer observation. On the contrary, the more we scrutinize that succession the more we are struck by the rigid uniformity, the punctual precision with which, wherever we can follow them, the operations of nature are carried on.

In the first passage only two words are of classical origin – 'peradventure' and 'mischief'. In the second nearly all the main verbs, nouns, and adjectives are from classical languages.

As a consequence of its borrowing from different languages, English is full of doublets and even triplets, synonyms which have come into the language from different sources. Sometimes we can choose between the old English word and one borrowed from French, Latin or Greek as in 'bodily' and 'corporeal', 'starry' and 'sidereal', 'doggy' and 'canine', 'catlike' and 'feline', 'learned' and 'erudite', 'help' and 'aid'. Sometimes we have a triple choice of the native term, one that has come from Latin but through French, and one that has come direct from Latin as 'kingly', 'royal', and 'regal', or 'end', 'finish', and 'conclude'.

The result of this richness of the English language is that the English writer has considerable linguistic choice and can select the word which has the precise nuance of meaning which he desires from a wide range of synonyms. You will remember that we defined a synonym as 'a word of *approximately* the same meaning'. Real synonymy – where one word is the exact equivalent of another – is very rare and is probably only to be found in a few technical terms. Practically all words have various differing shades of meaning, however slight. A test for absolute synonymy would be that one word could be substituted for another in all circumstances, and this is almost never possible. Professor Quirk illustrates how a word may be substituted for another in one context with negligible change of meaning but may cause considerable change in meaning in another. The words 'abnormal' and 'exceptional' in the meteorological semantic fields are interchangeable: 'The rainfall in April was exceptional' and 'The rainfall in April was abnormal' are not noticeably different in meaning. In the human context, however, there is a very big difference in meaning between 'My son is exceptional' and 'My son is abnormal'.

HOW WORDS DIFFER FROM EACH OTHER

How then do synonyms differ from one another when their references are almost identical? There can be differences in feeling-tone as we have already seen. Again one word may have more evocative value than another – a 'maiden' sounds more romantic than a mere 'girl', a 'casement' than a 'window'. A 'tome' suggests something not only physically larger and heavier than the average 'book' but with rather forbidding contents as well. It may simply be that one word tends to be used in certain contexts and not in others – what would be a 'staircase' on land becomes a 'companion-way' on a ship and we would proceed 'aft' rather than go 'to the back'.

This question of the peculiar qualities a word may have is, of course, one which is of great concern to the translator who is trying to convey in another language as close an impression as possible of the original work, and hence a good deal of work on the differences between synonyms has been done by people concerned with translations from one language to another.

Perhaps the simplest illustration of the importance of shades meaning in synonyms can be seen in the translation of the French verb *demander*, which simply means 'to ask'. It would be understandable but quite wrong to translate the French terms by the English word 'demand', since in English 'demand' has a much stronger and more forceful connotation than 'ask'. A diplomatic note from the French government which began 'La Gouvernement française demande une explication' would simply 'ask' for an explanation. If the phrase were wrongly translated as '*demands* an explanation', the false peremptory tone imported into the original might provoke an international incident.

Professor W. E. Collinson, who was concerned with the problem of how certain concepts in English would be handled in German, was forced to examine with some care how English synonyms differ from one another, and he suggested that there were at least nine different ways.

One term may be *general* and *inclusive* in its application while the other is more *specific* and *exclusive*: 'To go on foot' covers many activities such as march, hobble, limp, etc. One term is more *intense* than the other: 'repudiate' as contrasted with 'decline' or 'turn down' or 'reject'. Professor Collinson analyses in detail the shades of difference in these instances:

The word *decline* is associated with a certain degree of formality, of politeness and the observance of correct procedure. If *refuse* be taken as a neutral datum line, *decline* is situated on a higher level, but the next synonym *turn down* is on the lower level of colloquial speech barely emerging into written usage. As is the case with many colloquialisms, *turn down* is feeling-toned, for it conveys an attitude of independence and of resistance to persuasion. In the given context *reject* appears to be more peremptory; it often suggests a laconic, official or legal setting in which, of course, as in to *reject a bill* or a *motion* the word is devoid of any special feeling-component. *Repudiate* is the strongest term of all and implies an attitude of scorn, disgust, or righteous indignation.[1]

This illustrates excellently the area and range of choice which is available to the writer.

Again, one term may be more highly charged with emotion than the other, as we have already seen with 'repudiate' and 'decline'; or in 'civil servant' and 'bureaucrat'. Similarly one term may imply moral approbation or censure where another is neutral as in 'tight-fisted' or 'economical', 'eavesdrop' or 'listen'. The fifth suggested distinction is that one term is more 'professional' than another: the word 'decease' would be appropriate in a legal document where the more common term 'death' would be used elsewhere.

Further, one word may be more *literary* than another, more suited to the written language, and within the literary language there are further distinctions such as that one term may be more poetical or archaic or romantic than another. One might possibly refer to a Knight's 'steed' but a policeman's mount is more likely to be a plain 'horse'. In *Five Modern Authors* by J. I. M. Stewart, the last volume in the *Oxford History of English Literature*, the author says of Robert Louis Stevenson that 'his hair depended upon his shoulders'. Now while it is true that by derivation the word 'depend' does mean 'to hang down', it must be said that it is seldom used in this sense in modern English and the author is using it in an archaic sense.

The next category of distinctions is that some words are more *colloquial* than others, acceptable in conversation but possibly out of place or less acceptable in writing, and like the literary language, the spoken language itself contains further distinctions into the *familiar*, the *slangy*, and the *vulgar*. Within a language, again, some words are peculiar to a particular dialect or are restricted to a particular region, as in Scotland a 'butcher' is still occasionally called a 'flesher'. The final category in the classification is the one suggested by the terms used by children or adults talking to children. 'Father' is a fairly formal term, and therefore within the family circle 'daddy', 'dad', or 'papa', a warmer, more familiar term is normally used. Notice, too, in the last example how the choice of one of the three possibilities might well indicate the social class of the user as well.

---

[1] This was written in 1939. Do you think *turn down* would still be regarded as a colloquialism 'barely emerging into written usage'?

This classification does not claim to be complete in any way and further grounds for distinction could be discovered. It does indicate very clearly, however, how words differ in their quality, and it is the ability to select with discrimination within this field that marks the good writer, and the ability to recognize the discrimination that marks the perceptive reader.

TONE

When I. A. Richards produced his more subtle definition of meaning, he distinguished four different aspects of meaning which he designated sense, feeling, intention, and tone. The first three we have already considered: the sense is what any given passage refers to, its subject matter; the feeling is the emotive overtones of the passage; and the intention is the author's purpose in writing. The final aspect, tone, is of great importance and is itself determined to a large extent by the other three aspects of meaning.

The term itself is a metaphorical extension of the word we apply literally to the speaking voice. When we talk about the tone in which someone says something, we are referring to the quality of the sound that is used. The implication of a simple statement can be radically altered by changing the tone in which it is uttered. It can reveal anger or sympathy, resignation or exasperation, depending on whether it is uttered gently and kindly or brusquely and peremptorily.

Sometimes the variation in tone of voice is accompanied by variation in the form of the expression. A request for a book to be brought can range from the peremptory 'Bring me that book', through the polite 'Would you mind bringing me that book', to the effusive 'I would be so terribly grateful if you would be so very kind as to bring me that book', with all sorts of shades in between.

In the written word, of course, the author does not have the benefit of the quality of sound to convey the full implications of his meaning, nor the facial expressions and bodily gestures which may help to reinforce it. The only resources he has are the quality of the words he selects and the variations in the form of his sentences.

What particular tone a writer adopts will be determined principally by two things: the nature of his subject matter and the attitude he assumes towards his audience. The latter is of paramount importance for tone is essentially concerned with relationships between people. A person invited to deliver an address to a learned academic body or scientific society may introduce his paper with a few humorous remarks to catch his audience's attention at the outset, but he is unlikely to maintain a facetious tone throughout. In contrast a guest invited to deliver an after-dinner speech, when he can expect his audience to be in a relaxed and jovial mood and incapable of concentrating on deep intellectual matters for any length of time, is expected to sustain a fairly light and humorous tone throughout, although a certain amount of serious matter may be embedded in his discourse.

Tone, then, depends on the relationship between author and audience and subject matter. It will reveal itself largely in the writer's choice of grammatical structures and of vocabulary, particularly the latter. Take, for example, the following passage from Joseph Conrad's story *Youth*. The narrator is the person involved in the experience being described and he is telling the story long afterwards to some friends over a bottle of wine. Conrad therefore wants to establish a conversational tone, as of a man leisurely telling a story. The circumstances are that an old tramp-steamer has sprung a leak in a violent storm. The narrator, Marlow, is a young junior officer on board. After describing the exhausted crew pumping continuously to try to keep the ship afloat, Conrad continues:

And there was somewhere in me the thought: By Jove! This is the deuce of an adventure – something you read about; and it is my first voyage as second mate – and I am only twenty – and here I am lasting it out as well as any of these men, and keeping my chaps up to the mark. I was pleased. I would not have given up the experience for worlds. I had moments of exultation. Whenever the old dis-mantled craft pitched heavily with the counter high in the air, she seemed to throw up, like an appeal, like a defiance, like a cry to the clouds without mercy, the words written on her stern; 'Judea, London. Do or Die'.

O Youth! the strength of it, the faith of it, the imagination of it! To me she was not an old rattletrap carting about the world a lot of coal for freight – to me she was the endeavour, the test, the trial of life. I think of her with pleasure, with affection, with regret – as you would think of someone dead you have loved. I shall never forget her. . . . Pass the bottle.

The passage does, of course, contain a good deal of 'literary' language but carefully interspersed in it are the colloquialisms which give the impression of the speaking voice: 'By Jove!', 'deuce', 'my chaps', 'an old rattletrap carting about a lot of coal'. Conrad does not even hesitate

THE LANGUAGE OF PROSE

to introduce the flat cliché, 'I would not have given up the experience for worlds', since it is appropriate and reinforces the effect he is striving for.

The sentence structure too has the simple repetitive pattern of conversation; 'and' is used four times as a connective in the first sentence, and this is followed by three short simple sentences. The later sentences are longer but no more complex. The apostrophe to Youth seems rather rhetorical but the narrator is looking back with an ironic nostalgia to the time when danger could be accepted as a test of manhood. The introduction of the pronoun 'you' towards the end of the passage reminds us of his audience and finally, to bring them sharply into focus, comes the request, 'Pass the bottle'. Even the punctuation is designed to suggest the speaking voice as we can see from the number of times the dash is used.

In contrast to the Conrad passage, here is the beginning of a short story where, although the conversational familiar style is still marked, a significant difference in tone is used. Conrad's narrator is a mature adult looking back upon the idealism and openness to experience of Youth. John Updike's narrator in *A and P* is a young shop assistant in a supermarket in a small New England town.

In walks these three girls in nothing but bathing suits. I'm in the third checkout slot, with my back to the door, so I don't see them until they're over by the bread. The one that caught my eye first was the one in the plaid green two-piece. She was a chunky kid, with a good tan and a sweet broad soft-looking can with those two crescents of white just under it, where the sun never seems to hit, at the top of the backs of her legs. I stood there with my hand on a box of HiHo crackers trying to remember if I rang it up or not. I ring it up again and the customer starts giving me hell. She's one of these cash-register-watchers, a witch about fifty with rouge on her cheekbones and no eyebrows, and I know it made her day to trip me. She's been watching cash registers for fifty years and probably never seen a mistake before.

By the time I got her feathers smoothed and her goodies into a bag – she gives me a little snort in passing, if she'd been born at the right time they would have burned her over in Salem – by the time I get her on her way the girls had circled around the bread and were coming back, without a pushcart, back my way along the counters, in the aisle between the checkouts and the special bins. They didn't even have shoes on. There was this chunky one, with the two-piece –

it was bright green and the seams on the bra were still sharp and her belly was still pretty pale so I guessed she just got it (the suit) – there was this one, with one of those chubby berry-faces, the lips all bunched together under her nose, this one, and a tall one, with black hair that hadn't quite frizzed right, and one of those sunburns right across under the eyes, and a chin that was too long – you know, the kind of girl other girls think is very 'striking' and 'attractive' but never quite makes it, as they very well know, which is why they like her so much – and then the third one, that wasn't quite so tall.

Ever since Mark Twain wrote *Huckleberry Finn* in 1884, American writers have been masters of the informal, colloquial style as a literary medium and Updike shows that contemporary United States authors have not lost the touch. The tone is established immediately by the first sentence with its colloquial inversion of the Adjunct, Predicator, Subject, coupled with the grammatical solecism of the lack of concord between subject and verb. The narrator of this passage is obviously none too well educated. This impression is reinforced by the lack of consistency in the use of tenses, the speaker moving without apparent motive from present to past and back again. The present tense is used here in fact as a kind of historic present as it frequently is in popular colloquial speech. The rather naïve, artless character of the narration is further suggested by the number of digressions inserted in the sentences. The final sentence is a particularly good example of this where all three girls are described in one long digressive sentence. A more sophisticated narrator would almost certainly have split the sentence into three.

The vocabulary is in keeping with the sentence structure. Apart from the slang terms 'can', 'giving me hell', 'witch', and 'goodies', Updike makes clever use of the demonstrative adjectives 'this' (in the phrase 'There was this chunky one' or, in the plural, 'these three girls') in the sense of 'a certain', a use which occurs almost exclusively in conversation. Updike's narrator uses slang rather than the colloquialisms of Marlow.

His attitude to what he is writing about is different too. His comments on the customer whose purchase he rings up twice and the tall girl reveal a certain cynical outlook which is totally foreign to the Conrad passage.

Both of the passages we have been considering are from novels, but tone is equally important in non-fiction. The following two paragraphs form the introduction to Aldous Huxley's essay *Foreheads Villainous*

73

Low. The success of the essay is partly due to the tone achieved by Huxley.

In *A Farewell to Arms*, Mr Ernest Hemingway ventures, once, to name an Old Master. There is a phrase, quite admirably expressive (for Mr Hemingway is a most subtle and sensitive writer) a single phrase, no more, about 'the bitter nail-holes of Mantegna's Christs; then quickly, quickly, appalled by his own temerity, the author passes on (as Mrs Gaskell might hastily have passed on, if she had somehow been betrayed into mentioning a water-closet), passes on shamefacedly to speak once more of Lower Things.

There was a time, not so long ago, when the stupid and uneducated aspired to be thought intelligent and cultured. The current of aspiration has changed its direction. It is not at all uncommon now to find intelligent and cultured people doing their best to feign stupidity and to conceal the fact that they have received an education. Twenty years ago it was still a compliment to say of a man that he was clever, cultivated, interested in the things of the mind. Today 'highbrow' is a term of contemptuous abuse. The fact is surely significant.

These paragraphs, particularly the first, are good examples of the careful manipulation of tone. There is a lightness of touch but at the same time the tone, although relaxed, is not conversational. The sentences are too elegantly structured for that. The adverb 'once' is carefully placed in isolation after the verb instead of its more usual position before it in the first sentence. The singularity, in both senses of the term, of the phrase about Mantegna's Christs is emphasized again in the second sentence with the repetition of 'a phrase' and 'a single phrase, no more' and the appearance of the phrase itself is delayed while Huxley expresses his approbation of both the phrase and its author. The second part of the sentence has the same pattern of repetition separated by parenthesis (this time to introduce the analogy of the Victorian lady novelist in order to suggest that Hemingway felt some impropriety in making a cultural reference) and 'Lower Things' gets capitals on the analogy of 'Higher Things'.

Having caught the reader's attention with this striking concrete instance, Huxley goes on in the second paragraph in a more straightforward way to introduce the theme of his essay, contrasting the present and the near past. In all, the reader gets the impression of sophistication, urbanity, intelligence and wit. The title itself adds its quota to this impression since it is a quotation from Shakespeare's *Tempest*.

FIGURES OF SPEECH

In the examination of any piece of prose, it is, of course, essential to consider the effect of any of the linguistic devices known generally as Figures of Speech. In general it is true to say that poetry is more figurative than prose but figures of speech play an important part in the latter as well. The proportion of figurative language is likely to be highest in creative and imaginative prose and lowest in scientific. An extreme example is the Aeolus episode in Joyce's *Ulysses* which takes place in a newspaper office: Every episode in *Ulysses* is related to a certain Art and the appropriate one in this instance is Rhetoric, the art of the effective handling of language, since that is the journalist's main problem as a writer. Into this relatively short chapter of only thirty-two pages Joyce ingeniously wove examples of nearly every rhetorical device, not only the familiar ones such as simile and metaphor but a host of abstruse figures identified and classified by Aristotle and the medieval Schoolmen. Stuart Gilbert, Joyce's secretary, in his study of the novel was able to identify nearly a hundred separate examples without repetition and these by no means exhausted all the figures in the chapter.

We have already had occasion to refer to figures of speech, such as antithesis, in the chapter on the grammatical element, since they fall broadly into two categories: those which depend for their effect on arrangement, on syntactical patterns, and those which are dependent principally on meaning. It is the latter group that we are concerned with here, and particularly the two most frequent figures in prose, simile and metaphor. It would be quite impossible to examine all the figurative devices based on meaning but simile and metaphor require special attention.

Aristotle said in his *Poetics*, a treatise on rhetoric: 'The greatest thing by far is to have a command of metaphor. This alone cannot be imparted to another; it is the mark of genius, for to make good metaphors implies an eye for resemblances.' In Aristotle's sense of the term metaphor includes the simile and the metaphor proper, those figures of speech which depend on the recognition of similarities and differences between objects and events, and he rightly underlines their crucial importance in language.

In a sense it is a mistake to regard metaphor as simply one among a great number of rhetorical devices since it would seem to be the basis on which language grows and develops.

What is a metaphor? The dictionary definition is 'a figure of speech by which a thing is spoken of as being that which it only resembles'. In other words a term from one area of experience is transferred to another area of experience because some similarity has been observed between two objects or events. This metaphoric process is so fundamental to language that we are not normally conscious of it. When we read a sentence such as 'The village was situated at the foot of a mountain', we are not conscious that the word 'foot' is used metaphorically, but a transference has taken place from one area of experience, the human body, to another, the physical or geographical. The metaphor in this instance is in fact dead, the resemblance between the two terms no longer rising into consciousness. 'Foot' has simply taken on a new sense, the 'base' of something. The English language is full of these corporeal metaphors – the eye of a needle, the brow of a hill, the mouth of a river – and this would seem to point to one of the purposes of metaphor, that it allows us to deal with the new and the unfamiliar in terms of that which we already know.

Language is a storehouse of metaphor, and is constantly being extended and developed by this transference of a word from one area of experience to another. A single page of a newspaper provided the following: 'Britain will become a stagnant backwater'; 'The eleven-plus examination is a form of educational apartheid'; 'The war on want'; 'Scientist's breakthrough'; 'The Nottingham Theatre has established a bridge-head'; 'Peking Thaw over Formosa'.

I. A. Richards has introduced some useful critical terms for the discussion of metaphor. In any metaphor there are three things involved: the object or idea we are talking about, the term to which it is likened, and the common element, the similarity. These he calls the 'tenor', the 'vehicle' and the 'ground' respectively.

In an effective metaphor there must be a certain distance between the tenor and the vehicle, they must come from different areas of experience. We must be aware of the dissimilarities between the two as well as the similarity. If the two are too close together we do not get the pleasure of seeing both terms at once, as it were. While grasping the metaphor as a unity we are aware of the two separate elements which make up that unity and the tension that is created between them.

When a metaphor becomes dead we are no longer aware of both elements; one disappears and the other is left holding the field. The metaphorical sense has then become one of the recognized meanings of the word. The English language is full of dead and moribund metaphors. The important ones are those which are still vivid and fresh.

Broadly speaking, metaphors, and other figures of speech, serve two main purposes; they can have a logical or clarifying function or they can enhance the emotive impact. In some cases they combine both tasks. George Orwell's essay *Politics and the English Language* provides some excellent examples of the effective use of similes which both clarify and reinforce the emotional tone he is trying to maintain. Orwell believed that the effect of politics on the English language was disastrous, since stale clichés replaced precision of thought. The figures he used to describe this state of affairs exemplified the freshness and vividness he would have liked to see:

> Prose consists less and less of *words* chosen for the sake of their meaning and more and more of phrases *tacked* together *like the sections of a pre-fabricated henhouse.*

Or again:

> . . . the writer knows more or less what he wants to say, but an accumulation of stale phrases chokes him *like tea leaves blocking a sink.*

The inflated style he described as '. . . a kind of euphemism. A mass of Latin words falls upon the facts *like soft snow*, blurring the outline and covering up all the details,' and the motive behind it was that 'When there is a gap between one's real and one's declared aims, one turns as it were instinctively to long words and exhausted idioms, *like a cuttlefish squirting out ink*'.

In contrast to the spare functional effectiveness of Orwell's figures here is a passage from C. E. Montague on slang:

> Perfect slang has a cunning brevity that braces you. It should taste sweet and keen, like a nut. If it does, it will make its way yet into that holy of holies where 'literary' English lives in state: For this queenly figure has the instinctive sagacity of every successful ruling caste. She does not build the wall round her fastness too high; and she makes good the natural losses of her establishment by opening a postern gate now and then and letting in the pick of the lusty upstarts of the period. No assemblage of academic duennas, however august, can put the kibosh upon her when she is thus prudently minded. 'Me for it,' she will say, and turn the key, and take 'blurb' to her bosom.

This passage is clotted with figures of speech, but the principal one is the metaphor of the English language as a 'queenly figure'. The most noticeable point about it is the way the author is able to extend and elaborate the figure in detail once the initial comparison has been made. The tone in the Montague passage is quite different from Orwell's, being much lighter, not to say flippant, and the reader does perhaps get the impression of the author showing off a bit.

IMAGERY

Figures of speech might well be included under the last aspect of meaning now to be discussed – imagery. Imagery is a difficult term to define and we use it in the sense of any appeal to the senses in a literary work – all of them, not just the visual sense as the word would seem to imply. Images frequently occur in similes and metaphor and at one time the term 'imagery' was restricted to such figurative uses. Now, however, it includes any concrete appeal to the senses, literal as well as figurative.

The importance of imagery is that it can evoke atmosphere or suggest meanings without the author being explicit. Dickens was a master at using imagery which both provided an appropriate atmosphere and suggested a symbolic interpretation in the context of the particular novel. The images of crime and convicts and prison hulks which pervade *Great Expectations* and the fog which enshrouds the opening chapters of *Bleak House* are famous examples.

One of the supreme illustrations of the use of imagery to create a particular effect is the passage at the beginning of D. H. Lawrence's *The Rainbow* describing the relationship of the Brangwen family to nature. As farmers they live their lives in harmony with the rhythms of the seasons and Lawrence himself used the term 'blood intimacy' for this relationship:

So the Brangwens came and went without fear of necessity, working hard because of the life that was in them, not for the want of the money. Neither were they thriftless. They were aware of the last halfpenny, and instinct made them not waste the peeling of their apple, for it would help to feed the cattle. But heaven and earth was teeming around them, and how should this cease? They felt the rush of the sap in spring, they knew the wave which cannot halt, but every year throws forward the seed to begetting, and, falling back, leaves the young born on the earth. They knew the intercourse between heaven and earth, sunshine drawn into the breast and bowels, the rain sucked up in the daytime, nakedness that comes under the wind in autumn, showing the birds' nests no longer worth hiding. Their life and inter-relations were such; feeling the pulse and body of the soil, that opened to their furrow for the grain, and became smooth and supple after their ploughing, and clung to their feet with a weight that pulled like desire, lying hard and unresponsive when the crops were to be shorn away. The young corn waved and was silken, and the lustre slid along the limbs of the men who saw it. They took the udder of the cows, the cows yielded milk and pulse against the hands of the men, the pulse of the blood of the teats of the cows beat into the pulse of the hands of the men. They mounted their horses, and held life between the grip of their knees, they harnessed their horses at the wagon, and, with hand on the bridle-rings drew the heaving of the horses after their will.

It is almost entirely by the use of imagery that Lawrence suggests the union of the Brangwens with the organic world of nature. The fertility cycle is evoked at the beginning of the paragraph by the images aroused by words and phrases like 'the earth was teeming', 'the rush of the sap in spring', 'the seed to begetting', and 'the young born'. Then the imagery becomes more overtly sexual. One simply has to list the words with sexual connotations to see how Lawrence is manipulating the reader's responses: 'intercourse', 'breast', 'sucked', 'nakedness', 'opened to their furrow', 'a weight that pulled like desire', 'lying hard and unresponsive'. These are only some of the images which lie behind the description of the Brangwen's relationship to the soil. The reader inevitably sees it in terms of the intimate relationship between men and women.

Equally interesting, of course, are the rhythms of the passage. The simplicity of the language and the faintly Biblical rhythm of the sentences at the beginning suggest that the relationship of the Brangwens to the earth has a sacramental quality. The most obvious manipulation of rhythm occurs, however, in the description of the milking – 'the pulse of the blood of the teats of the cows beat into the pulse of the hands of the men' – where the succession of prepositional phrases reproduces the pulse beat.

By this subtle interplay of rhythm and imagery Lawrence succeeds in conveying the impression of the Brangwen men's intimacy with the rhythm of nature.

Exercises – Meaning

In the following passages your attention is directed to one particular aspect of meaning which seems worthy of special attention but you may, of course, wish to do a complete analysis.

Examine the *tone* of the following passages:

1. CYRIL: The theory is certainly a very curious one, but to make it complete you must show that Nature, no less than Life, is an imitation of Art. Are you prepared to prove that?

VIVIAN: My dear fellow, I am prepared to prove anything.

CYRIL: Nature follows the landscape painter, then, and takes her effects from him?

VIVIAN: Certainly. Where, if not from the Impressionists, do we get those wonderful brown fogs that come creeping down our streets, blurring the gas lamps and changing the houses into monstrous shadows? To whom, if not to them and their master, do we owe the lovely silver mists that brood over our river, and turn to faint forms of fading grace, curved bridge and swaying barge? The extraordinary change that has taken place in the climate of London during the last ten years is entirely due to a particular school of Art. You smile. Consider the matter from a scientific or a metaphysical point of view, and you will find that I am right. For what is Nature? Nature is no great mother who has borne us. She is our creation. It is in our brain that she quickens to life. Things are because we see them, and what we see, and how we see it, depends on the arts that have influenced us. To look at a thing is very different from seeing a thing. One does not see anything until one sees its beauty. Then, and then only, does it come into existence. At present people see fogs, not because there are fogs, but because poets and painters have taught them the mysterious loveliness of such effects. There may have been fogs for centuries in London. I dare say there were. But no one saw them, and so we do not know anything about them. They did not exist until Art had invented them. Now, it must be admitted, fogs are carried to excess. They have become the mere mannerisms of a clique, and the exaggerated realism of their method gives dull people bronchitis. Where the cultured catch an effect, the uncultured catch cold.

OSCAR WILDE, *The Decay of Lying*

2. Macbriar had scarce understood the purport of the words as first pronounced by the Lord President of the Council; but he was sufficiently recovered to listen and to reply to the sentence when uttered by the harsh and odious voice of the ruffian who was to execute it and at the last awful words, 'and this I pronounce for doom', he answered boldly – 'My Lords, I thank you for the only favour I looked for, or would accept at your hands, namely, that you have sent the crushed and maimed carcass, which has this day sustained your cruelty, to this hasty end. It were indeed little to me whether I perish on the gallows or in the prison-house; but if death, following close on what I have this day suffered, had found me in my cell of darkness and bondage, many might have lost the sight how a Christian man can suffer in the good cause. For the rest, I forgive you, my Lords, for what you have appointed and I have sustained – and why should I not? – Ye send me to a happy exchange – to the company of angels and the spirits of the just, for that of frail dust and ashes – Ye send me from darkness into day – from mortality to immortality – and, in a word, from earth to heaven! If the thanks, therefore, and the pardon of a dying man can do you good, take them at my hand, and may your last moments be as happy as mine!'

WALTER SCOTT, *Old Mortality*

3. Francis Bacon has been described more than once with the crude vigour of antithesis; but in truth such methods are singularly inappropriate to his most unusual case. It is not by the juxtaposition of a few opposites, but by the infiltration of a multitude of highly varied elements, that his mental composition was made up. He was no striped frieze; he was shot silk. The detachment of speculation, the intensity of personal pride, the uneasiness of nervous sensibility, the urgency of ambition, the opulence of superb taste – these qualities, blending, twisting, flashing together, gave to his secret spirit, the subtle and glittering superficies of a serpent. A serpent, indeed, might well have been his chosen emblem – the wise, sinuous, dangerous creature, offspring of mystery and the beautiful earth.

LYTTON STRACHEY, *Elizabeth and Essex*

4. Along the shoreward edge of the shallows the advancing clearness was full of strange, moonbeam-bodied creatures with fiery eyes. Here and there a larger pebble clung to its own air and was covered with a coat of pearls. The tide swelled in over the rain-pitted sand

and smoothed everything with a layer of silver. Now it touched the first of the stains that seeped from the broken body and the creatures made a moving patch of light, as they gathered at the edge. The water rose further and dressed Simon's coarse hair with brightness. The line of his cheek silvered and the turn of his shoulder became sculptured marble. The strange, attendant creatures, with their fiery eyes and trailing vapours, busied themselves round his head. The body lifted a fraction of an inch from the sand and a bubble of air escaped from the mouth with a wet plop. Then it turned gently in the water.

Somewhere over the darkened curve of the world the sun and moon were pulling; and the film of water on the earth planet was held, bulging slightly on one side while the solid core turned. The great wave of the tide moved further along the island and the water lifted. Softly, surrounded by a fringe of inquisitive bright creatures, itself a silver shape beneath the steadfast constellations, Simon's body moved out towards the open sea.

WILLIAM GOLDING, *Lord of the Flies*

5. The plowing, now in full swing, enveloped him in a vague, slow-moving whirl of things. Underneath him was the jarring, jolting, trembling machine; not a clod was turned, not an obstacle encountered, that he did not receive the swift impression of it through all his body; the very friction of the damp soil, sliding incessantly from the shining surface of the shears, seemed to reproduce itself in his fingertips and along the back of his head. He heard the horses' hoofs by the myriads crushing down easily, deeply, into the loam, the prolonged clinking of trace chains; the working of the smooth brown flanks in the harness; the clatter of wooden hames; the champing of bits; the click of iron shoes against pebbles; the brittle stubble of the surface ground cracking and snapping as the furrows turned; the sonorous, steady breaths wrenched from the deep, labouring chests, strap-bound, shining with sweat; and all along the line the voices of the men talking to the horses. Everywhere there were visions of glossy brown backs, straining, heaving, swollen with muscle; harness streaked with specks of froth; broad, cup-shaped hoofs heavy with brown loam; men's faces red with tan; blue overalls spotted with axle grease; muscled hands, the knuckles whitened in their grip on the reins; and through it all the ammoniacal smell of the horses, the bitter reek of perspiration of beasts and men, the aroma of warm leather,

the scent of dead stubble – and stronger and more penetrating than anything else, the heavy enervating odour of the upturned, living earth.

FRANK NORRIS, *The Octopus*

PART TWO

A Method of Attack

In Part One of this book you have been led through various aspects of prose writing. In Part Two we invite you to apply what you have learned to selected passages of expository and fictional prose. Your ultimate aim will be to produce a considered judgement, with the reasons for that judgement, upon the given passage. At this point we would remind you that whatever conclusions you may come to about the merits of a short excerpt of prose, you are not justified in applying your estimate of its worth to the *whole* work from which it has been torn. In evaluating a whole work, we must take into account many other, and higher, critical considerations that do not apply in the case of a short passage.

On approaching any piece of writing, we are about to engage in a new experience conveyed through language. Our close reading of a passage should reveal to us as much as possible of the author's expertise in the act of composing it, and as much as possible of his success or failure in achieving his writing aims.

We suggest one method of going about the task. You should read the passage twice at your normal speed, aiming at understanding the meaning of what it says. As you do so, by noting features of the vocabulary and grammatical structure, you might make a tentative estimate of the kind of writing the passage belongs to, and the kind of audience at which it seems to be directed. As an aid towards finding the full meaning you must also ask yourself such questions as:

1. What is the author's immediate purpose in penning this set of words?
2. What particular area of experience in fiction, or of subject in expository prose, is he revealing?
3. What attitude has he chosen to adopt towards his material?
4. What degree of intimacy is invited of his reader?

It may be that the answers are not of equal importance for judging the prose, or it may be that one or other of the questions is not capable of being answered. But if you can give answers, they will help to clarify your further reading of the passage.

Thereafter you are engaged in a detailed scrutiny of the excerpt noting all the devices of writing the author has employed and estimating why he has employed them and how successfully. In the end you should read the passage slowly, savouring in your mind the quality of the writing. You are then in a position to write an informed critical appreciation of the author's achievement.

To lead you towards the desired state in which you can tackle a prose excerpt on its own, we have graded the exercises.

In Group A we have provided, for each excerpt, a fairly large number of questions, designed to direct your attention to specific aspects of the writer's thought or techniques. Normally these will require only brief answers, though you should make as many valid points in each answer as you can.

In Group B we have generally reduced the number of questions, and thus the amount of direction given to you so that you will need to do more exploration on your own. Your answers will therefore have to be rather more expansive.

In Group C we have left the number of questions to a minimum. Your answers to such questions may involve you in a scrutiny of a number of details of various kinds and they should be fairly lengthy.

In Group D we merely give you a number of excerpts of which you have to give a critical appreciation without any guidance other than yourself and your acquired expertise.

As preparation for the ultimate aim of Group D, it is open to you, for any excerpt, once you have answered the questions, to write a critical appraisal of the writer's achievement.

Shortly after this a very melancholy occurrence took place. I had observed for some days past, as we proceeded north and the nights became shorter, that the cock we shipped at Stornoway had become quite bewildered on the subject of that meteorological phenomenon called the Dawn of Day. In fact, I doubt whether he ever slept for more 5
than five minutes at a stretch, without waking up in a state of nervous agitation, lest it should be cock-crow. At last when night ceased altogether, his constitution could no longer stand the shock. He crowed once or twice sarcastically, then went melancholy mad: finally, taking a calenture, he cackled lowly (probably of green fields), and leaping 10
overboard, drowned himself. The mysterious manner in which every day a fresh member of his harem used to disappear, may also have preyed upon his spirits.

LORD DUFFERIN, *Letters from High Latitudes*

1. What does 'this' in 'Shortly after this' indicate about the excerpt?
2. What expectation does the phrase 'a melancholy occurrence' (line 1) arouse?
3. How does the word 'cock' contrast with the quality of the verbs used in the second sentence?
4. What effect on the tone have the words 'that meteorological phenomenon' (line 4)?
5. What was the dilemma of the cock?
6. Discuss the humorous effect got from humanizing the cock?
7. Comment on the compression obtained by the grammatical structure of the second last sentence (lines 8–10).
8. Can you see the point of ('probably of green fields') (line 10)? If not, refer to *Henry V*, Act II Scene 3.
9. How does the language used in the final sentence contrast with the importance of what is being related?

And at the moment when the Queen was crowned the peeresses had
likewise put on their coronets, in a single gesture of exquisite beauty,
their white arms rising with a sound like the rushing of birds' wings
and a proud arching like the arching of the neck of a swan. Then out
5 came the little mirrors, and, with furtive peeps in that cluster of
femininity, hands had stolen upwards again to adjust, to straighten.
Many dowagers, looking down from the galleries above, tut-tutted. In
their day, they said, ladies were not in the habit of producing mirrors
in public. It was easy to see, they said, that the reign of Edward the
10 Seventh was over, and the days of decent behaviour ended.

Everybody streamed out of the Abbey, greatly relieved. They were
tired, but how impressive it had been. Groups of lord and ladies stood
about, chattering while they waited for their carriages. Incongruous
sights were to be observed: one backwoodsman peer had put on a
15 straw hat, which contrasted oddly with his robes; another had wrapped
his coronet in a piece of newspaper. Someone was saying that old
Lord ———— had placed his sandwiches loose in his coronet, and had
upset them all over his head at the moment of the crowning.

One by one the coaches, carriages, and cars rolled up and rolled away.
20 Sebastian found himself once more shut into his musty box, alone. He
pressed his hands to his head, where his coronet had weighed upon it.

v. SACKVILLE-WEST, *The Edwardians*

1. In the first paragraph there are three kinds of tone. Describe each one.
2. Choose those words that seem to you to contribute most towards
   establishing each tone.
3. How far is the second paragraph a development of the final sentence of
   the first paragraph?
4. Comment on the quality of incident selected in the second paragraph.
5. Comment on the grammatical devices and sound effects used in the first
   sentence of the last paragraph.
6. What effects are obtained by 'musty box, alone'?
7. Describe briefly the quality of the humour and try to account for it.

In our time it is broadly true that political writing is bad writing. Where it is not true, it will generally be found that the writer is some kind of rebel, expressing his private opinions and not a 'party line'. Orthodoxy, of whatever colour, seems to demand a lifeless, imitative style. The political dialects to be found in pamphlets, leading articles, 5 manifestos, White Papers and the speeches of under-secretaries do, of course, vary from party to party, but they are all alike in that one almost never finds in them a fresh, vivid, home-made turn of speech. When one watches some tired hack on the platform mechanically repeating the familiar phrases – *bestial atrocities, iron heel, bloodstained tyranny, free* 10 *peoples of the world, stand shoulder to shoulder* – one often has a curious feeling that one is not watching a live human being but some kind of dummy: a feeling which suddenly becomes stronger at moments when the light catches the speaker's spectacles and turns them into blank discs which seem to have no eyes behind them. And this is not altogether 15 fanciful. A speaker who uses that kind of phraseology had gone some distance towards turning himself into a machine. The appropriate noises are coming out of his larynx, but his brain is not involved as it would be if he were choosing his words for himself. If the speech he is making is one that he is accustomed to make over and over again, 20 he may almost be unconscious of what he is saying, as one is when one utters the responses in church, and this reduced state of consciousness, if not indispensable, is at any rate favourable to political conformity.

GEORGE ORWELL, Politics and the English Language

1. What do you think of the first sentence as the opening of an argument? Pay special attention to the grammatical position of 'In our time' and the use of 'broadly'.
2. How does the second sentence relate to 'broadly'.
3. In the sentence beginning 'When one watches' (line 8) what words of the author contrast with 'fresh, vivid, home-made' (line 8)?
4. In what way does the short sentence, 'And this is not altogether fanciful'. (line 15) act as a pivot in the structure of the argument?
5. How is the idea contained in 'blank discs' developed later in the passage?
6. Comment on the use of connectives in the last two sentences.
7. How successfully, for you, has the author made his point? Try to account for the degree of success.

A4

The small locomotive engine, number 4, came clanking, stumbling
down from Selston with seven full wagons. It appeared round the
corner with loud threats of speed, but the colt that it startled from
among the gorse, which still flickered indistinctly in the raw afternoon,
5 out-distanced it at a canter. A woman, walking up the railway line to
Underwood, drew back into the hedge, held her basket aside, and
watched the footplate of the engine advancing. The trucks thumped
heavily past, one by one, with slow inevitable movement, as she stood
insignificantly trapped between the jolting black wagons and the
10 hedge; then they curved away towards the coppice where the withered
oak leaves dropped noiselessly, while the birds pulling at the scarlet
hips beside the track, made off into the dusk that had already crept into
the spinney. In the open, the smoke from the engine sank and cleaved
to the rough grass. The fields were dreary and forsaken, and in the
15 marshy strip that led to the whimsey, a reedy pit-pond, the fowls had
already abandoned their run among the alders, to roost in the tarred
fowl-house. The pit-bank loomed up beyond the pond, flames like
red-sores licking its ashy sides, in the afternoon's stagnant light. Just
beyond rose the tapering chimneys and the clumsy black headstocks of
20 Brinsley Colliery. The two wheels were spinning fast up against the
sky, and the winding engine rapped out its little spasms. The miners
were being turned up.

D. H. LAWRENCE, Odour of Chrysanthemums

1. What characteristics of the engine are emphasized in the opening lines?
2. How does the writer diversify the grammatical structure of the first
   sentence, and to what effect?
3. What effects are gained by the introduction of the colt? How is it related
   to the locomotive?
4. The woman, like the colt, is affected by the locomotive. How do her
   reactions contrast with those of the colt?
5. Comment on 'insignificantly trapped'.
6. The first four sentences open grammatically with the subject. The fifth
   (line 13) has the adjunct in the thematic position. What change does this
   effect in the perspective of the story?
7. Comment on 'Just beyond' (line 18) as a linking device.
8. Comment on the sound of 'the trucks thumped heavily past, one by one,
   with slow inevitable movement' (lines 7–8).
9. Show by quotation how the writer blends the natural and the man-made,
   the beautiful and the ugly.

Hastily putting the horses under cover, he sought shelter beneath the lintel of the door, whence he could still observe the courtyard. The air was thicker now than ever, and such a steaming and droning rose from the downpour that no footfall of man or beast could be heard above it. The roads, pitted as they were with great holes, would be under water, 5 and perhaps impassable. But of what effect this would have upon their flight he scarcely thought. Suddenly, with an awful and ominous noise, a voice full of horror and alarm, which raised every hair of anguish in Orlando's soul, St Paul's struck the first stroke of midnight. Four times more it struck remorselessly. With the superstition of a lover 10 Orlando had made out that it was on the sixth stroke that she would come. But the sixth echoed away, and the seventh came, and the eighth, and to his apprehensive mind they seemed notes first heralding and then proclaiming death and disaster. When the twelfth struck he knew that his doom was sealed. Other clocks struck, jangling one after 15 another. The whole world seemed to ring with the news of her deceit and his derision. He was bitten by a swarm of snakes, each more poisonous than the last. He stood in the doorway in the tremendous rain without moving. The downpour rushed on. In the thick of it great guns seemed to boom. Huge noises, as of the tearing and rendering of 20 oak trees, could be heard. There were also wild cries and terrible inhuman groanings. But Orlando stood there immovable till Paul's clock struck two, and then, crying aloud with an awful irony, and all his teeth showing, 'Jour de ma vie!' he dashed the lantern to the ground, mounted his horse, and galloped he knew not where.

VIRGINIA WOOLF, *Orlando*

1. What words in the opening sentence suggest the story is set in a past age?
2. Comment on the kinds of effect obtained by the grammatical structure of the fourth sentence (lines 6–7)?
3. Look at the sentence beginning 'Suddenly' (line 7). How does the writer manage to charge the words 'St Paul's struck' with great force?
4. Comment on the use of sound in 'Four times more'.
5. Why was Orlando in an agitated frame of mind?
6. What effect is obtained by the short sentences from line 14 to line 22?
7. Comment on the last sentence as an end to the passage.
8. What was the 'awful irony' (line 23)?
9. Deal with one or two points at which the writer moves the reader from the exterior to the interior of the man's mind.

But at Balbo Avenue, just before Michigan Avenue reached the Hilton, the marchers were halted by the police. It was a long halt. Perhaps thirty minutes. Time for people who had been walking on the sidewalk to join the march, proceed for a few steps, halt with the others, wait,
5 get bored, and leave it. It was time for someone in command of the hundreds of police in the neighbourhood to communicate with his headquarters, explain the problem, time for the dilemma to be relayed, alternatives examined, and orders conceivably sent back to attack and disperse the crowd. If so, a trap was first set. The mules were allowed
10 to cross Balbo Avenue, then were separated by a line of police from the marchers, who now, several thousand compressed in this one place, filled the intersection of Michigan Avenue and Balbo. There, clammed by police on three sides, and cut off from the wagons of the Poor People's March, there, right beneath the windows of the Hilton
15 which looked down on Grand Park and Michigan Avenue, the stationary march was abruptly attacked. The police attacked with tear gas, with mace, and with clubs, they attacked like a chain saw cutting into wood, the teeth of the saw the edge of their clubs, they attacked like a scythe through grass, lines of twenty and thirty policemen
20 striking out in an arc, their clubs beating, demonstrators fleeing. Seen from overhead, from the nineteenth floor, it was like a wind blowing dust, or the edge of waves riding foam on the shore.

The police cut through the crowd one way, then cut through them another. They chased people into the park, ran them down, beat
25 them up; they cut through the intersection at Michigan and Balbo like a razor cutting a channel through a head of hair, and then drove columns of new police into the channel who in turn pushed out, clubs flailing, on each side, to cut new channels, and new ones again. As demonstrators ran, they reformed in new groups only to be chased by
30 the police again. The action went on for ten minutes, fifteen minutes, with the absolute ferocity of a tropical storm, and watching it from a window on the nineteenth floor, there was something of the detachment of studying a storm at evening through a glass, the light was a lovely gray-blue, the police had uniforms of sky-blue, even the ferocity had
35 an abstract elemental play of forces of nature at battle with other forces, as if sheets of tropical rain were driving across the street in patterns, in curving patterns which curved upon each other again.

NORMAN MAILER, *Miami and the Siege of Chicago*

1. What is the effect of 'But at Balbo Avenue' (line 1)?
2. What effect is obtained by the grammatical structure of the second and third sentences and the opening of the fourth sentence (lines 2–3)?
3. Get as much as you can from the way in which the word 'time' is used in connection with the halt.
4. Contrast the vocabulary of the fourth sentence (lines 3–5) with that of the fifth sentence (lines 5–9). What different effects result?
5. What function in the narrative structure does 'If so, a trap was first set' (line 9) have?
6. What response does the writer invite by his choice of similes?
7. Comment on the writer's use of repetition.
8. How does the writer suggest neutrality in the final sentence? Does he destroy his previous partisanship?
9. Contrast the use of the passive voice of verbs in connection with the marchers with the use of the active voice for the police. How does the choice affect the response of the reader?

'To work, Mary, to work,' cried the Collector, touching his wife on the shoulder with a switch.

Mrs Turton got up awkwardly. 'What do you want me to do? Oh, those purdah women! I never thought any would come. Oh dear?'

5 A little group of Indian ladies had been gathering in a third quarter of the ground, near a rustic summer-house in which the more timid of them had already taken refuge. The rest stood with their backs to the company and their faces pressed into a bank of shrubs. At a little distance stood their male relatives, watching the venture. The sight
10 was significant: an island bared by the turning tide, and bound to grow.

'I consider they ought to come over to me.'

'Come along, Mary, get it over.'

'I refuse to shake hands with any of the men, unless it has to be the Nawab Bahadur.'

15 'Whom have we so far?' He glanced along the line. 'M'm! h'm! much as one expected. We know why he's here, I think – over that contract, and he wants to get the right side of me for Mohurram, and he's the astrologer who wants to dodge the municipal building regulations, and he's that Parsi, and he's – Hullo! there he goes –
20 smash into our hollyhocks. Pulled the left rein when he meant the right. All as usual.'

'They ought never to have been allowed to drive in; it's so bad for them,' said Mrs Turton, who had at last begun her progress to the summer-house, accompanied by Mrs Moore, Miss Quested, and a
25 terrier. 'Why they come at all I don't know. They hate it as much as we do. Talk to Mrs McBryde. Her husband made her give purdah parties until she struck.'

'This isn't a purdah party,' corrected Miss Quested.

'Oh, really,' was the haughty rejoinder.

30 'Do kindly tell us who these ladies are,' asked Mrs Moore.

'You're superior to them, anyway. Don't forget that. You're superior to everyone in India except one or two of the Ranis, and they're on an equality.'

Advancing, she shook hands with the group and said a few words
35 of welcome in Urdu. She had learnt the lingo, but only to speak to her servants, so she knew none of the politer forms and of the verbs only the imperative mood. As soon as her speech was over, she inquired of her companions, 'Is that what you wanted?'

'Please tell these ladies that I wish we could speak their language,
40 but we have only just come to their country.'

'Perhaps we speak yours a little,' one of the ladies said.

'Why, fancy, she understands!' said Mrs Turton.

'Eastbourne, Piccadilly, Hyde Park Corner,' said another of the ladies.

'Oh, yes, they're English-speaking.' 45

'But now we can talk; how delightful!' cried Adela, her face lighting up.

'She knows Paris also,' called one of the onlookers.

'They pass Paris on the way, no doubt,' said Mrs Turton, as if she was describing the movements of migratory birds. Her manner had 50 grown more distant since she had discovered that some of the group were Westernized, and might apply her own standards to her.

E. M. FORSTER, A Passage to India

The above passage is a description of a 'Bridge' Party, held in India, to bridge the gap between the Indians and their English rulers during the time of the British Raj.

1. How does the author indicate the attitude of the collector and Mrs Turton to the whole proceedings at the beginning?
2. How does the author convey the shyness and reserve of the Indian ladies in the third paragraph?
3. How does the dialogue indicate the attitude of the Collector and his wife to their guests?
4. What impression do you receive of the character of Mrs Turton:

   (a) from her conversation?
   (b) from the author's comment?

5. Comment on the significance of 'lingo' (line 35) and 'she knew none of the politer forms and of the verbs only the imperative mood' (lines 36–7).

The stormy shores ran away right and left in straight lines, enclosing a sombre and rectangular pool. Brick walls rose high above the water – soulless walls, staring through hundreds of windows as troubled and dull as the eyes of over-fed brutes. At their base monstrous iron cranes
5 crouched, with chains hanging from their long necks, balancing cruel linking hooks over the decks of lifeless ships. A noise of wheels rolling over stones, the thump of heavy things falling, the racket of feverish winches, the grinding of strained chains, floated in the air. Between high buildings the dust of all the continents soared in short flights;
10 and a penetrating smell of perfumes and dirt, of spices and hides, of things costly and of many things filthy, pervaded the space, made for it an atmosphere precious and disgusting. The *Narcissus* came gently into her berth; the shadow of soulless walls fell upon her, the dust of all the continents leaped upon her deck, and a swarm of strange men,
15 clambering up her sides, took possession of her in the name of the sordid earth.

JOSEPH CONRAD, *The Nigger of the Narcissus*

1. What attitude has the writer towards the ship's docking?
2. What words suggest unpleasant associations. Detail these associations and account for their unpleasantness.
3. Trace the identification of the inanimate with living things, and comment.
4. How does the writer, by vocabulary and grammatical structures point up the idea of 'precious and disgusting' (line 12)?
5. Look at the final sentence. Now:

    (a) What is the effect of 'gently'?
    (b) How does the writer utilize ideas that have appeared before?
    (c) Contrast what comes before and after the semi-colon.
    (d) How does the writer gain the effect of an assault upon the ship? Quote to justify your answer.
    (e) Comment on the use of rhythm and grammatical structure.

Smoke was rising here and there among the creepers that festooned
the dead or dying trees. As they watched, a flash of fire appeared at
the root of one wisp, and then the smoke thickened. Small flames
stirred at the bole of the tree and crawled away through leaves and
brushwood, dividing and increasing. One patch touched a tree trunk   5
and scrambled up like a bright squirrel. The smoke increased, sifted,
rolled outwards. The squirrel leapt on the wings of the wind and
clung to another standing tree, eating downwards. Beneath the dark
canopy of leaves and smoke the fire laid hold on the forest and began
to gnaw. Acres of black and yellow smoke rolled steadily towards the 10
sea. At the sight of the flames and the irresistible course of the fire, the
boys broke into shrill, excited cheering. The flames, as though they
were a kind of wild life, crept as a jaguar creeps on its belly towards a
line of birch-like saplings that fledged an outcrop of the pink rock.
They flapped at the first of the trees, and the branches grew a brief 15
foliage of fire. The heart of flame leapt nimbly across the gap between
the trees and then went swinging and flaring along the whole row of
them. Beneath the capering boys a quarter of a mile square of forest
was savage with smoke and flame. The separate noises of the fire
merged into a drum-roll that seemed to shake the mountain.   20

WILLIAM GOLDING, *Lord of the Flies*

1. 'The squirrel leapt on the wings of the wind.' What does he really mean
   by 'The squirrel' here? How has he led us to accept this meaning?
2. How does he then develop the idea of 'The squirrel'?
3. How is the reaction of the boys made to suit the actions of a squirrel?
4. How and why does the writer continue with another animal?
5. Trace the movement of the ideas from 'Smoke was rising' (line 1) to
   'shake the mountain' (line 20).
6. Comment on the selection of finite verbs in lines 2 and lines 8.

Eleven o'clock. A knock at the door . . . I hope I haven't disturbed
you, madam. You weren't asleep – were you? But I've just given my
lady her tea, and there was such a nice cup over I thought, perhaps . . .
Not at all, madam. I always make a cup of tea last thing. She drinks
5 it in bed after her prayers to warm her up. I put the kettle on when she
kneels down and I say to it, 'Now you needn't be in too much of a
hurry to say your prayers.' But it's always boiling before my lady is
half through. You see, madam, we know such a lot of people, and
they've all got to be prayed for – every one. My lady keeps a list of
10 the names in a little red book. Oh dear! whenever someone new has
been to see us and my lady says afterwards, 'Ellen, give me my little
red book,' I feel quite wild, I do. 'There's another,' I think, 'keeping
her out of her bed in all weathers.' And she won't have a cushion, you
know, madam; she kneels on the hard carpet. It fidgets me something
15 dreadful to see her, knowing her as I do. I've tried to cheat her; I've
spread out the eiderdown. But the first time I did it – oh, she gave me
such a look – holy it was, madam. 'Did our Lord have an eiderdown,
Ellen?' she said. But – I was younger at the time – I felt inclined to
say, 'No, but our Lord wasn't your age, and he didn't know what it
20 was to have your lumbago.' Wicked – wasn't it? But she's too good,
you know, madam. When I tucked her up just now and seen – saw
her lying back, her hands outside and her head on the pillow – so
pretty – I couldn't help thinking, 'Now you look just like your dear
mother when I laid her out!'
25   . . . Yes, madam, it was all left to me. Oh, she did look sweet. I did
her hair, softlike, round her forehead, all in dainty curls, and just to
one side of her neck I put a bunch of the most beautiful purple pansies.
Those pansies made a picture of her, madam! I shall never forget
them. I thought tonight, when I looked at my lady, 'Now, if only the
30 pansies was there no one could tell the difference.'

                        KATHERINE MANSFIELD, *The Lady's Maid*

1. What are the linguistic devices used to show that this is spoken by a servant in the presence of a superior? Consider:
   (a) the dominant clause structure.

   (b) the use of connectives.
   (c) grammatical usage.
   (d) selection of vocabulary.

2. What different uses are made of the punctuation '. . . .' and the dash?
3. What is the character of the speaker? Is she honest and self-effacing or is she a calculating and sly minx? Quote to support your opinion.

B4

We can by no means agree with Sir John Malcolm, who is obstinately resolved to see nothing but honour and integrity in the conduct of his hero. But we can as little agree with Mr Mill, who has gone so far as to say that Clive was a man 'to whom deception, when it suited his purpose, never cost a pang'. Clive seems to us to have been constitutionally the very opposite of a knave, bold even to temerity, sincere even to indiscretion, hearty in friendship, open in enmity. Neither in his private life, nor in those parts of his public life in which he had to do with his countrymen, do we find any signs of a propensity to cunning. On the contrary, in all the disputes in which he was engaged as an Englishman against Englishmen, from his boxing-matches at school to those stormy altercations at the India House and in Parliament amidst which his later years were passed, his very faults were those of a high magnanimous spirit. The truth seems to have been that he considered Oriental politics as a game in which nothing was unfair. He knew that the standard of morality among the natives of India differed widely from that established in England. He knew that he had to deal with men destitute of what in Europe is called honour, with men who would give any promise without hesitation, and break any promise without shame, with men who would unscrupulously employ corruption, perjury, forgery, to compass their ends. His letters show that the great difference between Asiatic and European morality was constantly in his thoughts. He seems to have imagined, most erroneously in our opinion, that he could effect nothing against such adversaries, if he was content to be bound by ties from which they were free, if he went on telling truth, and hearing none, if he fulfilled, to his own hurt, all his engagements with confederates who never kept an engagement that was not to their advantage. Accordingly this man, in the other parts of his life an honourable English gentleman and soldier, was no sooner matched against an Indian intriguer, than he became himself an Indian intriguer, and descended, without scruple, to falsehood, to hypocritical caresses, to the substitution of documents, and to the counterfeiting of hands.

MACAULAY, *Essay on Clive*

1. The writer opens by rejecting two views of Clive. What were they? Comment on them.
2. Taking the sentence beginning 'The truth seems' (line 14) as the pivot of the argument what does the writer:

   (a) establish before this?
   (b) establish after this?

3. Explain how the final sentence relates to the structure of the argument already put forward.
4. Examine the writer's use of parallel grammatical structures. Estimate their effect on the reader's acceptance of the writer's argument.
5. Comment on the use of various kinds of sentence-linking devices and on the effect of the use of 'we' and 'us'.
6. Do you accept the writer's case? Justify your answer.

At intervals from the tops of one of the rare low swells of the land, Vanamee overlooked a wider horizon. On the other divisions of Quien Sabe the same work was in progress. Occasionally he could see another column of plows in the adjoining division – sometimes so close at
5 hand that the subdued murmur of its movements reached his ear; sometimes so distant that it resolved itself into a long brown streak upon the gray of the ground. Farther off to the west on the Osterman ranch other columns came and went, and once, from the crest of the highest swell on his division, Vanamee caught a distant glimpse of the
10 Broderson ranch. There, too, moving specks indicated that the plowing was under way. And farther away still, far off there beyond the fine line of the horizons, over the curve of the globe, the shoulder of the earth, he knew were other ranches, and beyond these others, and beyond these still others, the immensities multiplying to infinity.
15 Everywhere throughout the great San Joaquin, unseen and unheard, a thousand plows up-stirred the land; tens of thousands of shears clutched deep into the warm, moist soil.

It was the long stroking caress, vigorous, male, powerful, for which the earth seemed panting. The heroic embrace of a multitude of iron
20 hands, gripping deep into the brown, warm flesh of the land that quivered responsive and passionate under the rude advance, so robust as to be almost an assault, so violent as to be virtually brutal. There, under the sun and under the speckless sheen of the sky, the wooing of the Titan began, the vast, primal passion, the two world forces, the
25 elemental male and female, locked in a colossal embrace, at grapples in the throes of an infinite desire, at once terrible and divine, knowing no law, untamed, savage, natural, sublime.

FRANK NORRIS, *The Octopus*

1. In the first paragraph how does the writer obtain the following effects:

    (a) the movement from actuality to the imagination?
    (b) the gradually increasing scale of distance?

2. What does the second paragraph perform in the structure of the thought?
3. What has the imagery of the third paragraph in common with that of the passage from *The Rainbow* on pp. 78–9. In what respect does it differ?
4. Examine closely and comment on the vocabulary and structure of the last sentence of the passage.

Lytton Strachey was a humanist: he was interested in human motives and human eccentricities, awake to every instance of human absurdity or inconsistency. Like some skilful Jesuit confessor of the Baroque Age, he could explore, with seemingly infallible technique, every quaint recess and dark corner of the labyrinthine-human mind. But this 5
interest, this technique, so useful for the exposure of human behaviour, did not extend to the analysis of impersonal or social facts, which are also the material of history. To Strachey historical problems were always, and only, problems of individual behaviour and individual eccentricity. He read big biographies and wrote little biographies: 10
Boswell was the model for his reading, Aubrey for his writing; but historical problems, the problems of politics and society, he never sought to answer, or even to ask. He read the five volumes of Sir Theodore Martin's *Life of the Prince Consort*, and distilled from it every drop of essence that could possibly heighten the flavour of his own 15
work, but he skated timidly past the political significance of that patient, central, administrative career – its effect on the power of the Crown. He read the six volumes of Monypenny and Buckle's *Life of Disraeli* and contented himself with an incredibly superficial verdict. Because of a few personal eccentricities, Disraeli is dismissed as a mere 20
egotist, a vain, trivial figure of 'rococo futilities', an 'absurd Jew-boy' visible under all his trappings to the very end. Disraeli's political achievements – a social and political revolution silently achieved by brilliant tactics, under the forms of immutable conservatism – is never noticed: it is on a senile passion for Lady Bedford that the statesman's 25
whole career must finally be judged.

HUGH TREVOR ROPER, *Historical Essays*

1. How do the following words affect the presentation of ideas and the reader's response:
   (a) 'seemingly' (line 4).
   (b) 'But' (line 5).
   (c) 'and only' (line 9).
   (d) 'even to ask' (line 13).

2. Choose and comment on the condemnatory words and phrases by which the writer seeks to destroy Lytton Strachey as a historian.
3. Comment on the kind and quality of the concrete illustrations of Lytton Strachey's weakness.
4. Evaluate the writer's use of balance, contrast, and antithetical words in giving force to his case.

My father's first wife had died young, leaving a small girl. The widower's continued position as a son of the house, even after his marriage to my mother some ten years later on, was not looked upon as anomalous by anyone concerned; his octogenarian hosts had formed
5 the habit of seeing him as a member of their family. Their perceptions were not fine; and they were not struck by the extension of their hospitality, on the same terms, to my mother, her household, and her child. Their name was Merz. Arthur and Henrietta Merz. They were I believe second cousins, and belonged by descent to the Jewish upper-
10 bourgeoisie of Berlin, the Oppenheims and Mendelssohns and Simons, the dozen families or so whose money still came in from banking and from trade, but who also patronized and often practised the arts and sciences, and whose houses, with their musical parties and their pictures, had been oases in the Prussian capital for the last hundred
15 and twenty years. The Merzes were direct and not remote descendants of Henrietta Merz, the friend of Goethe and of Mirabeau, Schleier-macher, and the Humboldts, the woman who barely out of the ghetto set up a salon where she received the translators of Shakespeare with advice and the king of Prussia with reserve. This celebrated lady had
20 a tall figure and a Greek profile, a large circle, many lovers, and an enormous correspondence: like George Eliot, she spoke English, German, French, Italian, Spanish, Latin, Greek, and Hebrew, and unlike George Eliot she could also read in Swedish. No trace of this heredity survived in Grandmama and Granpapa Merz, the name I was
25 taught to give them when I learnt to speak and the only one, I find, I can now use with ease. They had no interests, tastes or thoughts beyond their family and the comfort of their persons. While members of what might have been their world were dining to the sounds of Schubert and of Haydn, endowing research and adding Corot land-
30 scapes to their Bouchers and the Delacroix, and some of them were buying their first Picasso, the Merzes were adding bell-pulls and thickening the upholstery. No music was heard at Voss Strasse outside the ball-room and the day nursery. They never travelled. They never went to the country. They never went anywhere, except to take a cure,
35 and then they went in a private railway carriage, taking their own sheets.

SYBILLE BEDFORD, *A Legacy*

1. This passage may be divided into three parts.

    (a) Where does the first part end? What does it establish?

    (b) Where does the second part end? What does it establish?

    (c) How are the ideas of the third part related to those in the first two parts?

2. Comment on:

    (a) 'Their name was Merz. Arthur and Henrietta Merz' (line 8).

    (b) 'were adding bell-pulls and thickening the upholstery' (lines 31–2).

    (c) 'taking their own sheets' (l. 35).

    (d) The effect of the structure of the sentences describing Henrietta Merz (lines 29–30).

    (e) The use of proper names.

    (f) The last four sentences (lines 32–6) as a fitting conclusion.

I ate the ham and eggs and drank the beer. The ham and eggs were in a round dish – the ham underneath and the eggs on top. It was very hot and at the first mouthful I had to take a drink of beer to cool my mouth. I was hungry and I asked the waiter for another order. I drank
5 several glasses of beer. I was not thinking at all but read the paper of the man opposite me. It was about the break through on the British front. When he realized I was reading the back of his paper he folded it over. I thought of asking the waiter for a paper, but I could not concentrate. It was hot in the café and the air was bad. Many of the
10 people at the tables knew one another. There were several card games going on. The waiters were busy bringing drinks from the bar to the tables. Two men came in and could find no place to sit. They stood opposite the table where I was. I ordered another beer. I was not ready to leave yet. It was too soon to go back to the hospital. I tried not to
15 think and to be perfectly calm. The men stood around but no one was leaving, so they went out. I drank another beer. There was quite a pile of saucers now on the table in front of me. The man opposite me had taken off his spectacles, put them away in a case, folded his paper and put it in his pocket and now sat holding his liqueur glass and looking
20 out at the room. Suddenly I knew I had to get back. I called the waiter, paid the reckoning, got into my coat, put on my hat and started out the door. I walked through the rain up to the hospital.

Upstairs I met the nurse coming down the hall.

'I just called you at the hotel,' she said. Something dropped inside me.
25 'What is wrong?'

'Mrs Henry has had a haemorrhage.'

'Can I go in?'

'No, not yet. The doctor is with her.'

'Is it dangerous?'
30 'It is very dangerous.' The nurse went into the room and shut the door. I sat outside in the hall. Everything was gone inside of me. I did not think. I could not think. I knew she was going to die and I prayed that she would not. Don't let her die. Oh, God, please don't
35 let her die. I'll do anything for you if you won't let her die. Please, please, please, dear God, don't let her die. Dear God, don't let her die. Please, please, please, don't let her die. God, please make her not die. I'll do anything you say if you don't let her die. You took the baby but don't let her die – that was all right but don't let her die. Please, please, dear God, don't let her die.

ERNEST HEMINGWAY, *A Farewell to Arms*

1. This passage divides itself into three parts, one narrative, one of dialogue and one of interior monologue, each with its own purpose. Consider each part in turn, commenting on

   (a) the intention of the novelist.
   (b) the choice and combination of ideas.
   (c) the grammatical structures employed.
   (d) other devices used.

2. If you have not already dealt in detail with the writer's use of short sentences, consider the different effects obtained by the writer's use of them in each part.

3. How well has the novelist related each part to the others?

The architect whose design was selected, both by the committee and by the Queen, was Mr Gilbert Scott, whose industry, conscientiousness, and genuine piety had brought him to the head of his profession. His lifelong zeal for the Gothic style having given him a special prominence, 5 his handiwork was strikingly visible, not only in a multitude of original buildings, but in most of the cathedrals of England. Protests, indeed, were occasionally raised against his renovations, but Mr Scott replied with such vigour and unction in articles and pamphlets that not a Dean was unconvinced, and he was permitted to continue his labours without 10 interruption. On one occasion, however, his devotion to Gothic had placed him in an unpleasant situation. The Government offices in Whitehall were to be rebuilt; Mr Scott competed, and his designs were successful. Naturally they were in the Gothic style, combining 'a certain squareness and horizontality of outline', with pillar-mullions, 15 gables, high-pitched roofs, and dormers; and the drawings, as Mr Scott himself observed, 'were perhaps the best ever sent in to a competition, or nearly so'. After the usual difficulties and delays the work was at last to be put in hand, when there was a change of Government and Lord Palmerston became Prime Minister. Lord Palmerston at once 20 sent for Mr Scott. 'Well, Mr Scott,' he said in his jaunty way. 'I can't have anything to do with this Gothic style. I must insist on your making a design in the Italian manner, which I am sure you can do very cleverly.' Mr Scott was appalled; the style of the Italian Renaissance was not only unsightly, it was positively immoral, and he sternly 25 refused to have anything to do with it. Thereupon Lord Palmerston assumed a fatherly tone. 'Quite true: a Gothic architect can't be expected to put up a Classical building; I must find some one else.' This was intolerable, and Mr Scott, on his return home, addressed to the Prime Minister a strongly worded letter, in which he dwelt upon 30 his position as an architect, upon his having won two European competitions, his being an A.R.A., a gold medallist of the Institute, and a lecturer on Architecture at the Royal Academy; but it was useless – Lord Palmerston did not even reply.

LYTTON STRACHEY, *Queen Victoria*

1. Show, by including quotations, how the writer purports to destroy the character and professional ability of Gilbert Scott.
2. How far does the writer really destroy Gilbert Scott *as an architect*?
3. How far does he destroy him *as a man*?
4. Choose, and comment on, three occasions in which irony is used.
5. What does the direct speech contribute to the effect of the passage?

C3

When a satellite-launching missile climbs away from the earth's surface, balanced on the tongue of flame from its rocket motor, it is beginning a process of parental self-sacrifice unequalled in the animal kingdom. In bringing the satellite to birth, the launching missile expends all the 5 power of its motors and consumes all but a tiny fraction of its own substance. Its exhausted husks drop back to earth, while the satellite begins a new life, flying on in black ingratitude. The launching process is for the satellite a short and violent introduction to a prolonged existence in orbit. But the satellite has not escaped from the earth's 10 grasp and, like all terrestrial creatures, it returns to earth, possibly as dust and ashes too, for a hot reception awaits it on re-entering the atmosphere.

This chapter describes each of the three phases of a satellite's life: launching; its long sojourn in orbit; and re-entry.

Launching phase

15 The aim of the launching process is to convey a satellite to the right place at the right speed, and before discussing the launching phase in detail we need to ask what speed is required, and why. A satellite in orbit is acted on by one force only, gravity, provided it is high enough to be free of air drag. Because of gravity, any object which is released 20 near the earth will drop about 16 feet in a time of one second. Suppose that you stand at the top of a cliff and drive a golf ball horizontally out to sea with a speed of, say, 100 ft per second: in one second it will travel 100 ft forward under the influence of your drive, and 16 ft down under the influence of gravity, as shown in Fig 1.i. If you wanted the 25 golf ball to become a satellite, you would have to find a cliff higher than the earth's atmosphere, and then drive the ball so fast that by the end of one second, when it has dropped 16 ft below its original horizontal line, it has reached a point where the sea beneath, which shares the earth's curvature, is 16 ft below *its* original horizontal. The 30 ball would then remain at the same height above the sea and circle the earth as a satellite. This situation is also shown in Fig. 1.i, though the height of the cliff would have to be much greater than 50 miles to avoid air drag completely.

DESMOND KING-HELE, *Satellites and Scientific Research*

1. The above passage is the opening of a work of scientific exposition. There is a marked difference between the style of the first paragraph and that of the second. Illustrate this difference by a detailed comparison of the first sentence of the first paragraph and the first sentence of *Launching Phase*.
2. Show how these characteristic features are continued in the prose that follows each of these sentences.
3. Give your opinion on the opening paragraph as the beginning of a serious scientific work.

'And div ye think to come here,' said Mause, her withered hand shaking in concert with her keen, though wrinkled visage, animated by zealous wrath, and emancipated, by the very mention of the test, from the restraints of her own prudence, and Cuddie's admonition –
5 'Div ye think to come here, wi' your soul-killing, saint-seducing, conscience-confounding oaths, and tests, and bands – your snares, and your traps, and your gins? – Surely it is in vain that a net is spread in the sight of any bird.'

'Eh! what, good dame?' said the soldier. 'Here's a whig miracle,
10 egad! the old wife has got both her ears and tongue, and we are like to be driven deaf in our turn. – Go to, hold your peace, and remember whom you talk to, you old idiot.'

'Whae do I talk to! Eh, sirs, ower weel may the sorrowing land ken what ye are. Malignant adherents ye are to the prelates, foul props to
15 a feeble and filthy cause, bloody beasts of prey, and burdens to the earth.'

'Upon my soul,' said Bothwell, astonished as a mastiff-dog might be should a hen-partridge fly at him in defence of her young, 'this is the finest language I ever heard! Can't you give us some more of it?'
20 'Gie ye some mair o't?' said Mause, clearing her voice with a preliminary cough, 'I will take up my testimony against you ance and again – Philistines ye are, and Edomites – leopards are ye, and foxes – evening wolves, that gnaw not the bones till the morrow – wicked dogs, that compass about the chosen – thrusting kine, and pushing
25 bulls of Bashan – piercing serpents ye are, and allied baith in name and nature with the great Red Dragon; Revelations, twalfth chapter, third and fourth verses.'

Here the old lady stopped, apparently much more from lack of breath than of matter.

SIR WALTER SCOTT, *Old Mortality*

1. What linguistic features of Mause's speech justify the soldier's comment 'the old wife has got . . . her . . . tongue'?
2. Show how Scott differentiates between the speech of Mause and the speech of the soldier. Quote to illustrate your answer.
3. Describe the features of Mause's speech that give it an invective quality.
4. Comment on the 'matter' of Mause's last speech. What does it reveal about her?

Ere introducing the scrivener, as he first appeared to me, it is fit I make some mention of myself, my *employés*, my business, my chambers, and general surroundings; because some such description is indispensable to an adequate understanding of the chief character about to be
5 presented.

Imprimis: I am a man who, from his youth upward, has been filled with a profound conviction that the easiest way of life is the best. Hence, though I belong to a profession proverbially energetic and nervous, even to turbulence, at times, yet nothing of that sort have I
10 ever suffered to invade my peace. I am one of those unambitious lawyers who never addresses a jury, or in any way draws down public applause; but in the cool tranquillity of a snug retreat, do a snug business among rich men's bonds and mortgages and title-deeds. All who know me, consider me an eminently *safe* man. The late John
15 Jacob Astor, a personage little given to polite enthusiasm, had no hesitation in pronouncing my first grand point to be prudence; my next method. I do not speak it in vanity, but simply record the fact, that I was not unemployed in my profession by the late John Jacob Astor; a name which, I admit, I love to repeat, for it hath a rounded
20 and orbicular sound to it, and rings like unto bullion. I will freely add, that I was not insensible to the late John Jacob Astor's good opinion.

Some time prior to the period at which this little history begins, my avocations had been largely increased. The good old office, now extinct in the State of New York, of a Master in Chancery, had been conferred
25 upon me. It was not a very arduous office, but very pleasantly remunerative. I seldom lose my temper; much more seldom indulge in dangerous indignation at wrongs and outrages; but I must be permitted to be rash here and declare that I consider the sudden and violent abrogation of the office of Master in Chancery, by the new
30 Constitution, as a ——— premature act; inasmuch as I had counted upon a life lease of the profits, whereas I only received those of a few short years. But this is by the way.

HERMAN MELVILLE, *Bartleby The Scrivener*

1. What evidence is there in the language and sentence structure of the passage that the narrator is a lawyer by profession?
2. What impression of the narrator's character do you obtain from the passage? Quote from the passage to justify your conclusions.
3. Comment on the statement, 'I belong to a profession proverbially, energetic and nervous, even to turbulence'.
4. Describe the tone of the passage.

It is told that such are the aerodynamics and wing-loading of the bumble-bee, that in principle, it cannot fly. It does, and the knowledge that it defies the august authority of Isaac Newton and Orville Wright must keep the bee in constant fear of a crack-up. One can assume, in
5 addition, that it is apprehensive of the matriarchy of which it is subject, for this is known to be an oppressive form of government. The bumble-bee is a successful but an insecure insect.

If all this be true, and its standing in physics and entomology is perhaps not of the highest, life among the bumble-bees must bear a
10 remarkable resemblance to life in the United States in recent years. The present organization and management of the American economy are also in defiance of the rules – rules that derive their ultimate authority from men of such Newtonian stature as Bentham, Ricardo and Adam Smith. Nevertheless there are occasions – the decade following World
15 War II was an example – when it works, and quite brilliantly. The fact that it does so, in disregard of precept, has caused men to suppose that all must end in a terrible smash. And, as with the bee, there is frequently a deep concern over the intentions of those in authority. This also leads to apprehension and insecurity.
20   It is with this insecurity, in face of seeming success, that this book, in the most general sense, is concerned. The favourable performance of the American economy in the years following World War II was a fact. There were some two million farm families, many of them in the southern Appalachians, who continued to live in a primitive and
25 anonymous squalor not surpassed in any country west of Turkey. There were urban slum dwellers and racial minorities, notably the Negroes, who could not view their lot with satisfaction. The same was true of those whose salaries, pension or dependence on past savings committed them to life on a fixed income. Elsewhere there was little
30 hardship. Nor, so far as one can judge, did the generality of Americans feel that their personal freedom had been seriously abridged. The ideas which caused the present to be viewed with such uncertainty, and the future with such alarm, were not operative. My purpose is to see why – and perhaps to learn how, if we are spared – these ideas can be kept
35 inoperative.

J. K. GALBRAITH, *American Capitalism*

1. In what way are the following ideas in the first paragraph used and developed in the second and third paragraphs:

   (a) 'it cannot fly' (line 2).
   (b) 'It does' (line 2).
   (c) 'fear of a crack up' (line 4).
   (d) 'apprehensive of the matriarchy' (line 5).
   (e) 'successful but insecure insect' (line 7).

2. What do you think of the first paragraph as the opening of a serious book on economics?
3. In what way, in the third paragraph, does he modify his description of the American economy as successful after World War II?
4. Comment on the tones of the writing in the passage and their appropriateness to the material.

C7

The new theory of matter, due particularly to J. J. Thomson and Lord Rutherford, began with the study of electric discharges in a high vacuum. This revealed a particle, the electron, much smaller than the atoms of chemistry. The study of radio-activity offered further evidence.
5 It was soon clear that chemical atoms could not be regarded as the final constituents of matter. Other sub-atomic particles, such as the proton, neutron and positron, appeared. The atom was neither solid nor simple. It seemed to be a complex structure, consisting mainly of empty space, and capable of disruption. This was not all. The discovery that the
10 ultimate particles of matter were smaller than had been supposed, though interesting, was not revolutionary. But the attempt to predict the behaviour of sub-atomic particles by Newtonian mechanics failed. This was serious. A new quantum mechanics had to be applied, which suggested that such particles were not definite things, in definite places,
15 having definite velocities. The mere act of observation affected their behaviour. It was impossible to know both the position and the velocity of an electron exactly, because measuring the one was liable to change the other. And, though electrons often behaved like particles, they seemed at times to exhibit interference as if they were groups of waves.
20 It was also found that mass could be annihilated with the appearance of an equivalent in radiation.

Thus the analysis of ordinary matter was apparently leading to something that differed *in kind* from ordinary matter. The ultimate particles seemed not to have those properties, such as performance, unique
25 positon, and amenability to Newtonian Law, which had come to be regarded as essential to all matter. Such properties now appeared to be statistical. They existed in large portions of matter (where the average behaviour of many particles was involved) but not in the individual particles. The accepted notion of matter, as something
30 simple and readily understood, was destroyed. It had to be admitted that matter was highly complex. Its constituent particles seemed to have incompatible properties, and no satisfactory physical picture of them could be formed.

L. W. H. HULL, *The History and Philosophy of Science*

1. The argument on the old and new conceptions of matter is developed in stages. Show how the following sentences mark off stages in the development of the exposition.

   (a) 'The atom was neither solid nor simple' (lines 7).
   (b) 'This was serious' (line 13).
   (c) 'Such properties now appeared to be statistical' (lines 26–7).

   State as briefly as you can what ideas lead to these conclusions.
2. Comment on the various devices used, particularly at the beginning of sentences, to link the thought of the passage.
3. Contrast this passage with the immediately preceding passage as a piece of expository prose.

The long-drawn booming of the wind in the wood and the sobbing and moaning in the maples and oaks near the house, had made Lettie restless. She did not want to go anywhere, she did not want to do anything, so she insisted on my just going out with her as far as the edge of the water. We crossed the tangle of fern and bracken, bramble and wild raspberry canes that spread in the open space before the house, and we went down the grassy slope to the edge of Nethermere. The wind whipped up noisy little wavelets, and the cluck and clatter of these among the pebbles, the swish of the rushes and the freshening of the breeze against our faces, roused us.

The tall meadow-sweet was in bud along the tiny beach and we walked knee-deep among it, watching the foamy race of ripples and the whitening of the willows on the far shore. At the place where Nethermere narrows to the upper end, and receives the brook from Strelley, the wood sweeps down and stands with its feet washed round with waters. We broke our way along the shore, crushing the sharp-scented wild mint, whose odour checks the breath, and examining here and there among the marshy places ragged nests of water-fowl, now deserted. Some slim young lapwings started at our approach, and sped lightly from us, their necks outstretched in straining fear of that which could not hurt them. One, two, fled cheeping into cover of the wood; almost instantly they coursed back again to where we stood, to dart off from us at an angle, in an ecstasy of bewilderment and terror.

D. H. LAWRENCE, *The White Peacock*

It was pitch dark and I couldn't see priest or anything else. Then I really began to be frightened. In the darkness it was a matter between God and me, and He had all the odds. He knew what my intentions were before I even started; I had no chance. All I had ever been told about confession got mixed up in my mind, and I knelt to one wall and said: 'Bless me, father, for I have sinned; this is my first confession'. I waited for a few minutes, but nothing happened, so I tried it on the other wall. Nothing happened there either. He had me spotted all right.

It must have been then that I noticed the shelf at about one height with my head. It was really a place for grown-up people to rest their elbows, but in my distracted state I thought it was probably the place you were supposed to kneel. Of course, it was on the high side and not very deep, but I was always good at climbing and managed to get up all right. Staying up was the trouble. There was room only for my knees, and nothing you could get a grip on but a sort of wooden molding a bit above it. I held on to the molding and repeated the words a little louder, and this time something happened all right. A slide was slammed back; a little light entered the box, and a man's voice said: 'Who's there?'

"'Tis me, father,' I said for fear he mightn't see me and go away again. I couldn't see him at all. The place the voice came from was under the molding about level with my knees, so I took a good grip of the molding and swung myself down till I saw the astonished face of a young priest looking up at me. He had to put his head on one side to see me, and I had to put mine on one side to see him, so we were more or less talking to one another upsidedown. It struck me as a queer way of hearing confessions, but I didn't feel it my place to criticize.

'Bless me, father, for I have sinned – this is my first confession,' I rattled off all in one breath, and swung myself down the least shade more to make it easier for him.

'What are you doing up there?' he shouted in an angry voice, and the strain the politeness was putting on my hold of the molding, and the shock of being addressed in such an uncivil tone, were too much for me. I lost my grip, tumbled, and hit the door an unmerciful wallop before I found myself flat on my back in the middle of the aisle. The people who had been waiting stood up with their mouths open. The priest opened the door of the middle box and came out, pushing his biretta back from his forehead; he looked something terrible. Then Nora came scampering down the aisle.

FRANK O'CONNOR, *First Confession*

Except for the Marabar caves – and they are twenty miles off – the city of Chandrapore presents nothing extraordinary. Edged rather than washed by the river Ganges, it trails for a couple of miles along the bank, scarcely distinguishable from the rubbish it deposits so freely. There are no bathing-steps on the river front, as the Ganges happens not to be holy here; indeed there is no river front, and bazaars shut out the wide and shifting panorama of the stream. The streets are mean, the temples ineffective, and though a few fine houses exist they are hidden away in gardens or down alleys whose filth deters all but the invited guest. Chandrapore was never large or beautiful but two hundred years ago it lay on the road between Upper India, then Imperial, and the sea, and the fine houses date from that period. The zest for decoration stopped in the eighteenth century, nor was it ever democratic. There is no painting and scarcely any carving in the bazaars. The very wood seems made of mud, the inhabitants of mud moving. So abased, so monotonous is everything that meets the eye, that when the Ganges comes down it might be expected to wash the excrescence back into the soil. Houses do fall, people are drowned and left rotting, but the general outline of the town persists, swelling here, shrinking there, like some low but indestructible form of life.

Inland the prospect alters. There is an oval Maidan, and a long sallow hospital. Houses belonging to Eurasians stand on the high ground by the railway station. Beyond the railway – which runs parallel to the river – the land sinks then rises again rather steeply. On the second rise is laid out the little civil station, and viewed hence Chandrapore appears to be a totally different place. It is a city of gardens. It is no city, but a forest sparsely scattered with huts. It is a tropical pleasance washed by a noble river. The toddy palms and neem trees and mangoes and pepul that were hidden behind the bazaars now become visible and in their turn hide the bazaars. They rise from the gardens where ancient tanks nourish them, they burst out of stifling purlieus and inconsidered temples. Seeking light and air, they soar above the lower deposit to greet one another with branches and beckoning leaves, and to build a city for the birds. Especially after the rains do they screen what passes below, but at all times, even when scorched or leafless, they glorify the city to the English people who inhabit the rise; so that newcomers cannot believe it to be so meagre as it is described, and have to be driven down to acquire disillusionment. As for the civil station itself, it provokes no emotion. It charms not, neither does it repel. It is sensibly planned with a red-brick club on its brow, and farther back a grocer's and a cemetery, and the bungalows are disposed along roads that intersect at right angles. It has nothing hideous in it, and only the view is beautiful; it shares nothing with the city except the overarching sky.

E. M. FORSTER, *A Passage to India*

The litigation had seemed interminable and had in fact been complicated; but by the decision on the appeal the judgement of the divorce-court was confirmed as to the assignment of the child. The father, who though bespattered from head to foot, had made good his case, was, in pursuance of this triumph, appointed to keep her: it was not so much that the mother's character had been more absolutely damaged as that the brilliancy of a lady's complexion (and this lady's, in court, was immensely remarked) might be more regarded as showing the spots. Attached, however, to the second pronouncement was a condition that detracted, for Beale Farange, from its sweetness – an order that he should refund to his late wife the twenty-six hundred pounds put down by her, as it was called, some three years before, in the interest of the child's maintenance and precisely on a proved understanding that he would take no proceedings: a sum of which he had had the administration and of which he could render not the least account. The obligation thus attributed to her adversary was no small balm to Ida's resentment; it drew a part of the sting from her defeat and compelled Mr Farange perceptibly to lower his crest. He was unable to produce the money or to raise it in any way; so that after a squabble scarcely less public and scarcely more decent than the original shock of battle his only issue from her predicament was a compromise proposed by his legal advisers and finally accepted by hers.

His debt was by this arrangement remitted to him and the little girl disposed of in a manner worthy of the judgement-seat of Solomon. She was divided in two and the portions tossed impartially to the disputants. They would take her, in rotation, for six months at a time; she would spend half the year with each. This was odd justice in the eyes of those who still blinked in the fierce light projected from the tribunal – a light in which neither parent figured in the least as a happy example to youth and innocence. What was to have been expected on the evidence was the nomination, in *loco parentis*, of some proper third person, some respectable, or at least some presentable friend. Apparently, however, the circle of the Faranges had been scanned in vain for any such ornaments; so that the only solution finally meeting all the difficulties was, save that of sending Maisie to a Home, the partition of the tutelary office in the manner I have mentioned.

HENRY JAMES, What Maisie Knew

The thief who had been knocked down had now recovered himself; and both together fell to belabouring poor Joseph with their sticks, till they were convinced they had put an end to his miserable being: they then stripped him entirely naked, threw him into a ditch, and departed with their booty.

The poor wretch, who lay motionless a long time, just began to recover his senses as a stage-coach came by. The postillion, hearing a man's groans, stopt his horses, and told the coachman he was certain there was a dead man lying in the ditch, for he heard him groan. 'Go on, sirrah,' says the coachman; 'we are confounded late and have no time to look after dead men.' A lady, who heard what the postillion said, and likewise heard the groan, called eagerly to the coachman to stop and see what was the matter. Upon which he bid the postillion alight, and look into the ditch. He did so and returned, 'that there was a man sitting upright, as naked as ever he was born'. – 'O J–sus,' cried the lady, 'a naked man! Dear coachman, drive on and leave him.' Upon this the gentlemen got out of the coach; and Joseph begged them to have mercy upon him: for that he had been robbed and almost beaten to death. 'Robbed!' cries an old gentleman: 'let us make all the haste imaginable, or we shall be robbed too.' A young man who belonged to the law answered, 'He wished they had passed by without taking any notice; but that now they might be proved to have been last in his company; if he should die they might be called to some account for his murder. He therefore thought it advisable to save the poor creature's life for their own sakes, if possible; at least if he died, to prevent the jury's findings that they fled for it. He was therefore of opinion to take the man into the coach, and carry him to the next inn.' The lady insisted, 'That he should not come into the coach. That if they lifted him in, she would herself alight: for she had rather stay in that place to all eternity than ride with a naked man.' The coachman objected, 'That he could not suffer him to be taken in unless somebody would pay a shilling for his carriage the four miles'. Which the two gentlemen refused to do. But the lawyer, who was afraid of some mischief happening to himself, if the wretch was left behind in that condition, saying no man could be too cautious in these matters, and that he remembered very extraordinary cases in the books, threatened the coachman and bid him deny taking him up at his peril; for that, if he died, he would be indicted for his murder; and if he lived, and brought an action against him, he would willingly take a brief in it. These words had a sensible effect on the coachman, who was well acquainted with the person who spoke them; and the old gentleman above mentioned, thinking the naked man would afford him frequent opportunities of showing his wit to the lady, offered to join with the company in giving a mug of beer for his fare; till, partly alarmed by the threats of the one, and partly by the promises of the other, and being perhaps a little moved with compassion at the poor creature's condition, who stood bleeding and shivering with the cold, he at length agreed; and Joseph was now advancing to the coach where, seeing the lady, who had the sticks of her fan before her eyes, he absolutely refused, miserable as he was, to enter, unless he was furnished with sufficient covering to prevent giving the least offence to decency; – so perfectly modest was this young man; such mighty effects had the spotless example of the amiable Pamela, and the excellent sermons of Mr Adams wrought upon him.

Though there were several great-coats about the coach, it was not easy to get over this difficulty which Joseph had started. The two gentlemen complained they were cold, and could not spare a rag; the man of wit saying, with a laugh, that charity began at home; and the coachman, who had two great-coats spread under him, refused to lend either, lest they should be made bloody: the lady's footman desired to be excused for the same reason, which the lady herself, notwith-standing her abhorrence of a naked man, approved: and it is more than probable poor Joseph, who obstinately adhered to his modest resolution, must have perished, unless the postillion (a lad who hath been since transported for robbing a henroost) had voluntarily stript off a great-coat, his only garment, at the same time swearing a great oath (for which he was rebuked by the passengers), 'That he would rather ride in his shirt all his life than suffer a fellow-creature to lie in so miserable a condition'.

HENRY FIELDING, *Joseph Andrews*